Salads

Mixed seafood salad, p. 202

Chicken Waldorf salad, p. 232

Sautéed duck salad with thyme & honey, p. 256

Spelt salad with tomatoes & feta, p. 122

Garbanzo bean salad with tzatziki dressing, p. 88

Classic rice salad, p. 168

Jumbo shrimp salad, p. 198

Mango with berries, p. 286

Couscous with eggplant, p. 124

ELENA BALASHOVA

Salads

Delicious Recipes for a Healthy Life

Reader's Digest

THE READER'S DIGEST ASSOCIATION, INC.
New York, New York / Montreal / Singapore

A READER'S DIGEST BOOK
This edition published by
The Reader's Digest Association, Inc.
by arrangement with McRae Books Srl

This book was created and produced by
McRae Books Srl
via Umbria, 36 - 50145 Florence, Italy
info@mcraebooks.com

FOR MCRAE BOOKS
Project Director Anne McRae
Art Director Marco Nardi
Photography Brent Parker Jones (R&R
PhotoStudio)
Text Elena Balashova
Dietitian Penny Doyle
Editing Lesley Robb
Food Styling Lee Blaylock, Michelle Finn
Food Preparation Michelle Finn
Layouts Aurora Granata
Prepress Filippo Delle Monache

FOR READER'S DIGEST
U.S. Project Editor: Andrea Chesman
Canadian Project Manager:
Pamela Johnson
Senior Art Director: George McKeon
Executive Editor, Trade Publishing:
Dolores York
Associate Publisher, Trade Publishing:
Rosanne McManus
President and Publisher, Trade Publishing:
Harold Clarke

LIBRARY OF CONGRESS
CATALOGING-IN-PUBLICATION DATA

Balashova, Elena, 1954–
  Salads : delicious recipes for a healthy life /
Elena Balashova.
    p. cm.
  Includes index.
  ISBN 978-1-60652-197-7 (U.S. Edition)
  ISBN 978-1-60652-198-4 (international
edition)
  1. Salads. I. Reader's Digest Association.
  II. Title.
TX740.B342 2011
641.8'3–dc22

2010019440

We are committed to both the quality of
our products and the service we provide to
our customers. We value your comments,
so please feel free to contact us.

The Reader's Digest Association, Inc.
Adult Trade Publishing
Reader's Digest Road
Pleasantville, NY 10570-7000

For more Reader's Digest products and
information, visit our websites:

www.rd.com (in the United States)
www.readersdigest.ca (in Canada)
www.rdasia.com (in Asia)

Printed in China

1 3 5 7 9 10 8 6 4 2

NOTE TO OUR READERS
Eating eggs or egg whites that are not
completely cooked poses the possibility
of salmonella food poisoning. The risk is
greater for pregnant women, the elderly,
the very young, and persons with impaired
immune systems. If you are concerned
about salmonella, you can use reconstituted
powdered egg whites or pasteurized eggs.

The level of difficulty for each recipe is given on a scale from
1 (easy) to 3 (complicated).

Contents

Introduction

Nutrition experts all agree—you should eat five or more servings of fruits and vegetables every day. Evidence suggests that the risk of developing many serious diseases, including type 2 diabetes, cancer, and heart disease, is reduced by eating more fruit and vegetables. Brimming with essential vitamins, minerals, phytochemicals, and dietary fiber, salads are among the healthiest food choices you can make.

Not only are salads healthy, but they are also colorful, versatile, and delicious. Here you will find more than 140 recipes for everything from light and leafy appetizers to hearty one-dish "salad meals." Almost all of them are easy and quick to prepare.

Light salads are perfect for getting trim in spring and great in summer when just the thought of being in the kitchen makes you break out in a sweat. But salads can also be nourishing in the cool of fall and bracing in the dead of winter. When the weather cools down, try our Spelt salad with tomatoes & feta, Sautéed duck with thyme & honey, or Warm steak salad with papaya & onion.

If you are not already a salad freak, now is the time to start. And here is the perfect book to get you on your way!

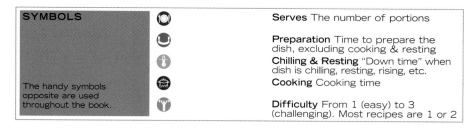

SYMBOLS		
	🍽	**Serves** The number of portions
	⬛	**Preparation** Time to prepare the dish, excluding cooking & resting
	🌡	**Chilling & Resting** "Down time" when dish is chilling, resting, rising, etc.
	⏲	**Cooking** Cooking time
The handy symbols opposite are used throughout the book.	🍸	**Difficulty** From 1 (easy) to 3 (challenging). Most recipes are 1 or 2

opposite: chicken, bean & arugula salad, p. 234

choosing a salad

This book has more than 140 recipes for scrumptious salads—something for everyone, and every occasion. But, what if you only have a few minutes or just a handful of ingredients in the refrigerator? The EASY section on the next page will solve the first problem and the JUST A FEW INGREDIENTS on page 14 will solve the second. Are you on a diet? See our LIGHT suggestions. See also the ONE-DISH MEALS, INTERNATIONAL, and EDITOR'S CHOICE recommendations.

LIGHT

asparagus & tomato salad with cucumber dressing, p. 18

arugula, corn & kiwi fruit salad, p. 42

spinach, grapefruit & pecorino salad, p. 48

summer greens with lime & cilantro p. 76

apple salad with yogurt dressing, p. 24

arugula & bread salad, p. 38

berry fruit salad, p. 302

fusilli & curry salad p. 140

classic rice salad, p. 168

mixed beans with tuna, p. 192

calabrian salad, p. 170

pork fillet & apple salad
p. 268

crunchy lentil salad, p. 96

warm potato & salmon
salad, p. 220

mixed seafood salad, p.
202

fruit salad with lemon
syrup, p. 284

mango with berries, p. 286

INTERNATIONAL

shrimp & mango salad,
p. 206

lamb & orange couscous
salad, p. 274

italian salad, p. 56

thai fish & mango salad
p. 218

rice noodle salad, p. 134

JUST A FEW INGREDIENTS

watermelon salad, p. 74

mozzarella & tomato
salad, p. 60

watercress & pear salad,
p. 80

arugula & pineapple salad,
p. 58

champagne strawberries,
p. 298

rice salad with apple & walnuts, p. 164

pasta salad with tomatoes, basil & cheese, p. 146

chicken, bean & arugula salad, p. 234

spelt salad with tomatoes & feta p. 122

lamb salad with herbs, p. 278

EDITOR'S CHOICE

roast beets with balsamic vinegar, p. 66

panzanella with tomato vinaigrette, p. 132

warm steak salad with papaya & onion, p. 272

blue cheese potato salad, p. 174

jumbo shrimp salad p. 198

chicken salad with prune vinaigrette p. 240

eggplant salad with prosciutto, p. 258

Light
& Leafy

asparagus & tomato salad
with cucumber dressing

 Serves 4

 15 minutes

 1 hour

 3–5 minutes

 1

CUCUMBER DRESSING

1   small cucumber, peeled, seeds removed, and cut into chunks

1   scallion (spring onion), coarsely chopped

Salt and freshly ground black pepper

2   tablespoons freshly squeezed lemon juice

1   tablespoon sour cream

¼   cup (60 ml) extra-virgin olive oil

2   tablespoons finely chopped fresh dill

SALAD

2   bunches asparagus, tough ends trimmed

4   small ripe tomatoes, peeled, halved, and seeds removed

2   cups (100 g) mixed salad greens

1. **To prepare the cucumber dressing,** combine the cucumber and scallion in a colander and sprinkle with salt. Leave to drain for 1 hour.

2. **Rinse** the cucumber and scallion mixture in cold water and drain again thoroughly.

3. **Purée** in a food processor. With the motor running, add salt, pepper, lemon juice, sour cream, and oil and process until smooth and creamy. Stir in the dill and chill in the refrigerator until ready to serve.

4. **To prepare the salad,** cook the asparagus in lightly salted boiling water until just tender, 3–5 minutes. Cut into 2-inch (5-cm) pieces.

5. **Cut** the tomatoes into strips. Arrange the salad greens on serving plates.

6. **Toss** the asparagus and tomato in the dressing and arrange over the salad greens on each plate.

AMOUNT PER SERVING	166 CALORIES 8%	3g PROTEIN 7%	15g FAT 19%	2g FIBER 8%	5g CARBS 4%	0.2 SALT 4%
NUTRITION FACTS PERCENT DAILY VALUES (based on 2000 calories)						

If you liked this recipe, you will love these as well.

warm fennel & asparagus **salad**

34

spring salad

72

summer greens with lime & cilantro

76

avocado, feta & bacon salad

Serve this salad with plenty of freshly baked bread as a starter or light lunch.

- Serves 6
- 15 minutes
- 6–7 minutes

2

4	cups (200 g) mixed salad greens
8	ounces (250 g) feta cheese, cubed
2	ripe avocados, peeled, pitted, and sliced
5	tablespoons freshly squeezed lemon juice
5	tablespoons extra-virgin olive oil
8	ounces (250 g) bacon, rinds removed, thinly sliced and cut into strips
	Pinch of sugar

1. **Arrange** the salad greens in a salad bowl. Add the feta and toss lightly.

2. **Put** the avocados in a small bowl and drizzle with the lemon juice. Set aside.

3. **Heat** 2 tablespoons of the oil in a large frying pan over medium heat. Add the bacon and fry until crisp and golden brown, about 5 minutes. Drain on paper towels, then add to the salad bowl.

4. **Drain** the avocados, reserving the lemon juice. Add the avocados to the salad bowl.

5. **Pour** the reserved lemon juice into the frying pan. Add the remaining oil and the sugar to the pan. Cook over medium-high heat for 1–2 minutes, scraping the bottom of the pan to incorporate the flavor of the bacon.

6. **Drizzle** the hot dressing over the salad, toss well, and serve.

AMOUNT PER SERVING	342	14g	31g	1g	2g	2.9g
NUTRITION FACTS	CALORIES	PROTEIN	FAT	FIBER	CARBS	SALT
PERCENT DAILY VALUES (based on 2000 calories)	16%	30%	38%	4%	2%	52%

If you liked this recipe, you will love these as well.

melon, zucchini & pancetta **salad**

28

spelt salad with tomatoes & feta

122

blue cheese & pecan salad

Creamy sweet Italian Gorgonzola cheese is perfect in this salad. Roquefort and Stilton are also good choices. The French bread (baguette) can be replaced with ciabatta, if preferred.

 Serves 4

 15 minutes

 5 minutes

 1

SALAD

½ loaf French bread

4 ounces (125 g) blue cheese, cut or crumbled into chunks

2 large, ripe pears, halved, cored, and thinly sliced

1 bunch arugula (rocket)

1 cup (125 g) roasted pecans

DRESSING

5 tablespoons (75 ml) extra-virgin olive oil

2 tablespoons freshly squeezed lemon juice

Salt and freshly ground black pepper

1. **To prepare the salad,** preheat the oven to 350°F (180°C/gas 4). Cut the French bread in half lengthwise, then tear into small pieces. Bake until golden and crisp, about 5 minutes.

2. **Put** the arugula in four individual serving bowls. Arrange the French bread and pears on top. Top with the pecans and cheese.

3. **To prepare the dressing,** whisk the oil and lemon juice in a small bowl. Season with salt and pepper.

4. **Drizzle** a little of the dressing over each salad and serve.

AMOUNT PER SERVING	771	20g	54g	5g	62g	2.1g
NUTRITION FACTS	**CALORIES**	**PROTEIN**	**FAT**	**FIBER**	**CARBS**	**SALT**
PERCENT DAILY VALUES (based on 2,000 calories)	37%	43%	67%	20%	48%	39%

If you liked this recipe, you will love these as well.

cheese, pear & kiwi fruit salad

26

pear, roquefort & radicchio salad

32

pasta salad with tomatoes, basil & cheese

146

apple salad with yogurt dressing

If preparing this salad ahead of time, squeeze the juice of 1 lemon over the slices of apple to prevent them from turning brown.

 Serves 6

 10 minutes

 1

SALAD

1	head romaine (cos) lettuce, coarsely chopped or torn
1	red apple, cored and cut into thin wedges
1	green apple, cored and cut into thin wedges
1	small head celery, sliced
⅓	cup (50 g) coarsely chopped walnuts

DRESSING

⅓	cup (90 ml) low-fat yogurt
⅓	cup (90 ml) mayonnaise
1	tablespoon Dijon mustard
1	tablespoon cider vinegar

1. **To prepare the salad,** put the lettuce in a large salad bowl. Add the apples, celery, and walnuts.

2. **To prepare the dressing,** whisk the yogurt, mayonnaise, and mustard in a small bowl. Add the vinegar and whisk again.

3. **Drizzle** the dressing over the salad. Serve at once.

AMOUNT PER SERVING	273	4g	25g	2g	8g	0.4g
NUTRITION FACTS	**CALORIES**	**PROTEIN**	**FAT**	**FIBER**	**CARBS**	**SALT**
PERCENT DAILY VALUES (based on 2 000 calories)	13%	9%	31%	8%	6%	8%

If you liked this recipe, you will love these as well.

apple, nut & celery **salad**

40

rice salad with apple & walnuts

164

chicken waldorf salad

232

cheese, pear & kiwi fruit salad

This light and refreshing salad can be served in late fall and winter when the new season's pears arrive in the markets.

Serves 6

15 minutes

1

SALAD

3 ripe kiwi fruit, peeled and cut into small cubes

2 large ripe pears, peeled, cored, and cut into cubes

12 ounces (350 g) Fontina, Edam, or other mild cheese, cut into small cubes

3 cups (150 g) mixed salad greens

¼ cup (45 g) golden raisins (sultanas)

DRESSING

⅓ cup (90 ml) extra-virgin olive oil

3 tablespoons balsamic vinegar

½ teaspoon cumin seeds (optional)

Salt and freshly ground black pepper

1. **To prepare the salad,** combine the kiwi fruit, pears, cheese, salad greens, and golden raisins in a large salad bowl.

2. **To prepare the dressing,** whisk the oil, vinegar, and cumin, if using, in a small bowl. Season with salt and pepper.

3. **Drizzle** the dressing over the salad, toss well, and serve.

AMOUNT PER SERVING	385 CALORIES	17g PROTEIN	29g FAT	2g FIBER	16g CARBS	1.4g SALT
NUTRITION FACTS PERCENT DAILY VALUES (based on 2000 calories)	19%	37%	36%	8%	12%	25%

If you liked this recipe, you will love these as well.

asparagus & tomato salad with cucumber dressing

18

blue cheese & pecan salad

22

26 LIGHT & LEAFY

melon, zucchini & pancetta salad

Pancetta is an Italian deli meat cut from the belly of the pig. Unlike bacon, it is not smoked. If unavailable, replace with bacon.

 Serves 4

 15 minutes

10 minutes

5 minutes

 1

4	ounces (125 g) pancetta, cut into thin strips
2	medium zucchini (courgettes), very thinly sliced lengthwise
	Freshly squeezed juice of $\frac{1}{2}$ lemon
1	cantaloupe (rock) melon, peeled, seeded, and cubed
$\frac{1}{2}$	honeydew melon, peeled, seeded, and cubed
1	small bunch frisée (curly endive), coarsely shredded
	Salt and freshly ground black pepper
$\frac{1}{3}$	cup (90 ml) extra-virgin olive oil
	Fresh mint leaves, to garnish

1. **Sauté** the pancetta in a small frying pan over medium heat until crisp and golden, about 5 minutes. Remove from the heat and set aside.

2. **Arrange** the slices of zucchini on a large plate. Drizzle with the lemon juice and let rest for 10 minutes.

3. **Place** both types of melon in a large salad bowl with the zucchini, pancetta, and endive. Toss gently.

4. **Arrange** the salad on four serving dishes. Season with salt and pepper and drizzle with the oil. Garnish with the mint and serve.

AMOUNT PER SERVING	300	9g	22g	3g	19g	1.1g
NUTRITION FACTS	CALORIES	PROTEIN	FAT	FIBER	CARBS	SALT
PERCENT DAILY VALUES (based on 2000 calories)	14%	20%	27%	2%	15%	19%

If you liked this recipe, you will love these as well.

avocado, feta & bacon salad

20

watermelon salad

74

kiwi fruit & mushroom salad

Kiwi fruit are an excellent source of vitamin C and potassium. They are low in calories and rich in dietary fiber. They make a healthy addition to salads in the winter.

Serves 4

15 minutes

10 minutes

1

- 1/3 cup (50 g) hazelnuts
- 4 slices bread, crusts removed and cubed
- 1 clove garlic, lightly crushed but whole
- 1/4 cup (60 ml) extra-virgin olive oil
- 4 cups (200 g) mixed salad greens

- 12 button mushrooms, thinly sliced
  Salt and freshly ground black pepper
- 4 ounces (125 g) Parmesan cheese, in shavings
- 2 ripe kiwi fruit, peeled and thinly sliced

1. **Preheat** the oven to 400°F (200°C/gas 6). Spread the hazelnuts on a baking sheet and toast until lightly browned, about 5 minutes. Let cool slightly.

2. **Sauté** the bread with the garlic in 2 tablespoons of oil in a small frying pan over medium heat until crisp and golden brown, about 5 minutes. Drain the croutons on paper towels. Discard the garlic.

3. **Combine** the salad greens and mushrooms in a large bowl. Drizzle with the remaining oil and season with salt and pepper. Toss well.

4. **Divide** the salad among four serving dishes. Top with the Parmesan, kiwi fruit, hazelnuts, and croutons and serve.

AMOUNT PER SERVING	437	18g	32g	3g	21g	1g
NUTRITION FACTS	CALORIES	PROTEIN	FAT	FIBER	CARBS	SALT
PERCENT DAILY VALUES (based on 2000 calories)	21%	39%	40%	12%	16%	18%

If you liked this recipe, you will love these as well.

mushroom & spinach salad

62

lettuce & grapefruit salad

70

pear, roquefort & radicchio
salad

If preferred, replace the Roquefort with another sharp, tasty blue cheese.

Serves 4

15 minutes

1

SALAD

2 large ripe pears, halved and cored

Freshly squeezed juice of 1 lemon

2 small heads green or red radicchio, coarsely chopped

4 ounces (125 g) Roquefort cheese, cut into cubes

20 walnuts, coarsely chopped

1 tablespoon snipped fresh chives

DRESSING

1/3 cup (90 ml) extra-virgin olive oil

2 tablespoons cider vinegar

1 teaspoon whole-grain mustard

1 shallot, finely chopped

Salt and freshly ground black pepper

1. **To prepare the salad,** cut the pears into thin wedges and drizzle with the lemon juice to prevent them from turning brown.

2. **Put** the pears, radicchio, Roquefort, and walnuts in a large salad bowl.

3. **To prepare the dressing,** whisk the oil, vinegar, mustard, and shallot in a small bowl. Season with salt and pepper.

4. **Drizzle** the salad with the dressing and toss gently. Sprinkle with the chives and serve.

AMOUNT PER SERVING	565	12g	55g	3g	7g	1.3g
NUTRITION FACTS	CALORIES	PROTEIN	FAT	FIBER	CARBS	SALT
PERCENT DAILY VALUES (based on 2000 calories)	27%	26%	68%	12%	5%	24%

If you liked this recipe, you will love these as well.

favorite caesar salad

52

mozzarella & tomato salad

60

warm fennel & asparagus salad

If pancetta is not available, replace with the same quantity of bacon (rinds removed.)

Serves 4

15 minutes

15 minutes

1

1/4 cup (60 ml) extra-virgin olive oil

4 medium tomatoes, thinly sliced

12 asparagus spears, tough stems removed and cut in half lengthwise

2 small bulbs fennel, cut in thin wedges

4 ounces (125 g) pancetta, thinly sliced

1 bunch baby spinach leaves
Salt

1 tablespoon green peppercorns in brine, rinsed

3 tablespoons balsamic vinegar

1. **Heat** 1 tablespoon of oil in a large frying pan over medium heat. Add the tomatoes and sauté for 1–2 minutes. Divide the tomatoes among four serving dishes.

2. **Cook** the asparagus and fennel in salted boiling water for 2–3 minutes. Drain well. Place the asparagus over the tomatoes. Set the fennel aside.

3. **Add** the pancetta to the frying pan used to cook the tomatoes and sauté over medium heat until crisp and golden, about 5 minutes. Set aside.

4. **Put** the fennel in the same frying pan over medium-high heat and sauté in the juices left by the tomatoes and bacon for 3–4 minutes.

5. **Arrange** the spinach on top of the tomatoes and asparagus. Top with the fennel. Season with salt and sprinkle with the green peppercorns.

6. **Drizzle** with the remaining oil and balsamic vinegar. Top with the pancetta and serve warm.

AMOUNT PER SERVING	248	13g	19g	5g	8g	1.6g
NUTRITION FACTS	CALORIES	PROTEIN	FAT	FIBER	CARBS	SALT
PERCENT DAILY VALUES (based on 2000 calories)	12%	28%	23%	20%	6%	29%

If you liked this recipe, you will love these as well.

pinzimonio

50

green pea salad

54

italian salad

56

orange & artichoke salad

Artichokes are a good source of dietary fiber, vitamin C, folate, and magnesium. They can be served raw or blanched in boiling water for 1 minute to soften a little.

Serves 4

15 minutes

1

4	artichokes
	Freshly squeezed juice of 1 lemon
2	oranges, peeled and divided into segments
5	ounces (150 g) aged pecorino cheese, flaked

1	tablespoon finely chopped fresh parsley
1/3	cup (90 ml) extra-virgin olive oil
	Salt and freshly ground black pepper

1. **Clean** the artichokes by trimming the stalks and cutting off the top third of the leaves. Remove the tough outer leaves by pulling them down and snapping them off at the base. Cut the artichokes in half and use a sharp knife to remove any fuzzy core. Cut the artichokes into thin wedges.

2. **Put** the artichokes in a large salad bowl and drizzle with half the lemon juice. This will stop them from turning brown.

3. **If liked,** blanch the artichokes in boiling water for 1 minute. Drain well, and let cool a little.

4. **Place** the oranges, pecorino, and parsley in a large salad bowl. Drain the artichokes and add to the bowl.

5. **Drizzle** with the oil and remaining lemon juice and season with salt and pepper. Toss gently and serve.

AMOUNT PER SERVING	374 CALORIES 18%	16g PROTEIN 35%	32g FAT 40%	1g FIBER 4%	8g CARBS 6%	0.7g SALT 13%
NUTRITION FACTS PERCENT DAILY VALUES (based on 2 000 calories)						

If you liked this recipe, you will love these ones too:

pinzimonio

50

bean salad with artichokes

84

middle eastern bean & artichoke salad

100

arugula & bread salad

This bread salad, inspired and loosely based on Tuscan panzanella (see page 132 for a modern version of this Italian classic), makes a hearty appetizer or light lunch.

Serves 6

20 minutes

45 minutes

5 minutes

1

14	ounces (400 g) firm-textured bread, thickly sliced	
2	cloves garlic	
4	large firm-ripe tomatoes, coarsely chopped	
	Salt	
⅓	cup (90 ml) extra-virgin olive oil	
	Freshly squeezed juice of 1 lemon	
1	small bunch fresh basil, torn	

Freshly ground black pepper

1 sweet red onion, finely chopped

1 cucumber, peeled and diced

1 green celery heart, coarsely chopped

12 large black olives, pitted and chopped

1 bunch arugula (rocket)

1. **Toast** the bread under the broiler (grill). Rub all over with the garlic, let cool, and cut into cubes.

2. **Put** the tomatoes in a colander and sprinkle with salt. Let drain for 15 minutes.

3. **Whisk** 5 tablespoons of oil, the lemon juice, basil, salt, and pepper in a small bowl.

4. **Combine** the bread, tomatoes, onion, cucumber, celery, olives, and arugula in a salad bowl.

5. **Drizzle** with the oil and lemon juice mixture and toss well.

6. **Let stand** for 30 minutes before serving.

AMOUNT PER SERVING	331	7g	17g	3g	41g	1.7g
NUTRITION FACTS	CALORIES	PROTEIN	FAT	FIBER	CARBS	SALT
PERCENT DAILY VALUES (based on 2000 calories)	16%	15%	21%	12%	32%	31%

If you liked this recipe, you will love these as well.

arugula & pineapple salad

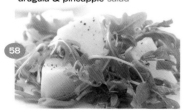
58

panzanella with tomato vinaigrette

132

bread salad with poached trout

196

apple, nut & celery salad

Crisp and tangy, this salad is full of energizing fruit and nuts.

 Serves 4

10 minutes

 1

2	large crisp Granny Smith apples, peeled, cored, and cut into bite-size pieces
¼	cup (60 ml) freshly squeezed lemon juice
6	stalks celery, trimmed and cut into bite-sized pieces
2	cloves garlic, finely chopped
½	cup (60 g) raisins
1	teaspoon cumin seeds
6	tablespoons finely chopped fresh parsley
1	cup (150 g) toasted salted nuts (peanuts, almonds, walnuts, cashews)
	Freshly ground black pepper
⅓	cup (90 ml) extra-virgin olive oil

1. **Put** the apples in a salad bowl. Drizzle with half the lemon juice to stop them from turning brown.

2. **Add** the celery, garlic, raisins, cumin, parsley, and nuts to the salad bowl.

3. **Season** with pepper and drizzle with the remaining lemon juice and the oil. Toss well and serve.

AMOUNT PER SERVING	486	9g	41g	4g	22g	0.1g
NUTRITION FACTS	CALORIES	PROTEIN	FAT	FIBER	CARBS	SALT
PERCENT DAILY VALUES (based on 2000 calories)	23%	20%	51%	16%	17%	2%

If you liked this recipe, you will love these as well.

apple salad with yogurt dressing

24

watercress & pear salad

80

rice salad with apple & walnuts

164

arugula, corn & kiwi fruit salad

This unusual combination of fruit and salad greens is packed with vitamins and minerals. Serve with fresh creamy cheeses and newly baked bread.

 Serves 4

🕙 10 minutes

🍽 1

2	bunches arugula (rocket)
1	cup (150 g) canned corn (sweet corn), drained
4	kiwi fruit, peeled and sliced
20	cherry tomatoes, cut in half
2	cloves garlic, finely chopped
1	fresh red chile, seeded and thinly sliced (optional)

Salt and freshly ground black pepper

⅓ cup (90 ml) extra-virgin olive oil

¼ cup (60 ml) balsamic (or white wine) vinegar

1. **Put** the arugula in a large salad bowl or in four individual salad bowls.

2. **Add** the corn, kiwi fruit, tomatoes, garlic, and chile, if using.

3. **Season** with salt and pepper and drizzle with the oil and vinegar.

4. **Toss** well and serve.

AMOUNT PER SERVING	296	3g	21g	3g	24g	0.3g
NUTRITION FACTS	CALORIES	PROTEIN	FAT	FIBER	CARBS	SALT
PERCENT DAILY VALUES (based on 2 000 calories)	14%	7%	26%	12%	18%	5%

If you liked this recipe, you will love these as well.

arugula & pineapple salad

58

chicken, bean & arugula salad

234

summer salad of grilled chicken, spinach & mango

244

wild salad greens with pancetta & balsamic vinegar

This is a classic Italian salad, traditionally made with wild salad greens gathered in the fields. Use any combination of in-season, locally grown salad greens.

Serves 4

10 minutes

5 minutes

4	cups (200 g) mixed salad greens
2	tablespoons butter
4	ounces (125 g) pancetta, cut in small dice

2	cloves garlic, finely chopped
¼	cup (60 ml) balsamic vinegar
	Salt and freshly ground black pepper

1

1. **Put** the salad greens in a large salad bowl or four individual bowls.

2. **Melt** the butter in a large frying pan over medium heat. Add the pancetta and garlic and sauté until the pancetta is crisp and golden, about 5 minutes.

3. **Add** the balsamic vinegar and season lightly with salt and pepper. Remove from the heat.

4. **Drizzle** the pancetta and butter mixture over the salad greens and serve immediately before the salad starts to wilt.

AMOUNT PER SERVING	107	6g	6g	1g	6g	1g
NUTRITION FACTS	**CALORIES**	**PROTEIN**	**FAT**	**FIBER**	**CARBS**	**SALT**
PERCENT DAILY VALUES (based on 2 000 calories)	5%	13%	7%	4%	5%	18%

If you liked this recipe, you will love these as well.

summer greens with lime & cilantro

76

eggplant salad with prosciutto

258

potato & smoked sausage salad

262

raspberry, feta & walnut salad

The fresh raspberries add an attractive touch of color to this light salad. For a change, substitute with 1 cup (about 150 g) chopped fresh pineapple pieces.

Serves 6

15 minutes

5 minutes

1

SALAD

4	ounces (125 g) walnuts
4	cups (200 g) mixed salad greens
8	ounces (250 g) feta cheese, crumbled
1	cup (150 g) fresh raspberries

DRESSING

2	scallions (spring onions), finely chopped
2	teaspoons spicy mustard
2	tablespoons raspberry vinegar
1	tablespoon balsamic vinegar
2	tablespoons honey
2	tablespoons freshly squeezed orange juice
½	cup (125 ml) extra-virgin olive oil

1. **To prepare the salad,** preheat the oven to 350°F (180°C/gas 4). Put the walnuts on a baking sheet and toast until crisp and golden, about 5 minutes. Let cool, then chop coarsely.

2. **To prepare the dressing,** combine the scallions, mustard, and both vinegars in a medium bowl. Add the honey and orange juice and whisk well. Add the oil a little at a time, whisking constantly.

3. **Put** the salad greens in a large salad bowl and toss with half the dressing.

4. **Divide** the salad greens among six serving dishes, and top each one with feta cheese, raspberries, and walnuts.

5. **Pour** the remaining dressing into a small bowl and pass separately at the table.

AMOUNT PER SERVING	CALORIES	PROTEIN	FAT	FIBER	CARBS	SALT
NUTRITION FACTS	453	11g	42g	2g	10g	1.4g
PERCENT DAILY VALUES (based on 2000 calories)	22%	24%	52%	8%	8%	26%

If you liked this recipe, you will love these as well.

kiwi fruit & mushroom salad

30

arugula, corn & kiwi fruit salad

42

lettuce & grapefruit salad

70

spinach, grapefruit & pecorino salad

If preferred, substitute the pecorino cheese with the same quantity of Parmesan.

 Serves 4

10 minutes

 1

SALAD

2	bunches baby spinach leaves
4	ounces (125 g) aged pecorino cheese, in shavings
1	grapefruit, peeled and divided into segments

DRESSING

⅓	cup (90 ml) extra-virgin olive oil
	Freshly squeezed juice of ½ lemon
1	tablespoon finely chopped fresh chives
	Salt and freshly ground black pepper

1. **To prepare the salad,** put the spinach on four individual serving plates. Top with the pecorino and grapefruit.

2. **To prepare the dressing,** whisk the oil, lemon juice, and chives in a small bowl. Season with salt and pepper.

3. **Drizzle** the dressing over the salads and serve.

AMOUNT PER SERVING	326	12g	30g	1g	3g	0.6g
NUTRITION FACTS	**CALORIES**	**PROTEIN**	**FAT**	**FIBER**	**CARBS**	**SALT**
PERCENT DAILY VALUES (based on 2000 calories)	16%	26%	37%	4%	2%	12%

If you liked this recipe, you will love these as well.

lettuce & grapefruit salad

70

couscous with oranges & pistachios

126

new mexico chicken salad

246

pinzimonio

This is a classic Tuscan dish, a sort of do-it-yourself salad that is served as an antipasto or to accompany a main course. Vary the vegetables according to the season. If desired, add a little red wine vinegar or balsamic vinegar to the dressing.

Serves 6

30 minutes

1

SALAD

4   artichokes
     Freshly squeezed juice
     of 2 lemons
4   carrots (or 8 baby carrots)
2   bunches celery
2   fennel bulbs
12   scallions (spring onions)
12   radishes

DRESSING

1   cup (250 ml) extra-virgin
     olive oil
     Salt and freshly ground
     black pepper

1. **To prepare the artichokes,** remove the tough outer leaves by pulling them down and snapping them off at the base. Cut off the stem and the top third of the leaves. Cut in half lengthwise and scrape any fuzzy choke away with a knife. Cut each artichoke into wedges and drizzle with the juice of 1 lemon. If desired, blanch the artichokes in boiling water for 1 minute. Drain well, and let cool a little.

2. **To prepare the carrots,** cut into long thin sticks and soak in a bowl of cold water with the remaining lemon juice for 10 minutes.

3. **To prepare the celery,** trim off the leafy tops and discard the tough outer stalks. Keep the inner white stalks and the heart.

4. **To prepare the fennel,** slice off the base, trim away the leafy tops, and discard any blemished outer leaves. Divide into six to eight wedges, depending on the size.

5. **To prepare the scallions,** remove the roots and the outer leaves and trim the tops.

6. **To prepare the radishes,** cut the roots off and trim the tops.

7. **To prepare the dressing,** whisk the oil with the salt and pepper until well mixed. Pour into six small bowls.

8. **To serve,** arrange the vegetables on a platter in the middle of the table and give each guest a plate and a small bowl of dressing.

AMOUNT PER SERVING	211	3g	19g	3g	8g	0.2g
NUTRITION FACTS	CALORIES	PROTEIN	FAT	FIBER	CARBS	SALT
PERCENT DAILY VALUES (based on 2000 calories)	10%	7%	23%	12%	6%	4%

favorite caesar salad

This is yet another variation on an old favorite. If you don't like anchovies, just leave them out of the dressing.

Serves 4

30 minutes

10 minutes

1

SALAD

2	thick slices bread, cut into cubes
2	tablespoons extra-virgin olive oil
	Salt and freshly ground black pepper
6	large thin slices prosciutto
1	head romaine (cos) lettuce
4	hard-boiled eggs, peeled and quartered
2	ounces (60 g) Parmesan cheese, in shavings

DRESSING

1/4	cup (60 ml) extra-virgin olive oil
2	tablespoons light (single) cream
4	salt-cured anchovy fillets
	Freshly squeezed juice of 1 1/2 lemons
2	cloves garlic, finely chopped
	Dash of Worcestershire sauce
1	teaspoon Dijon mustard
1	tablespoon white wine vinegar

1. **To prepare the salad,** preheat the oven to 425°F (220°C/gas 7). Arrange the bread on a baking sheet. Drizzle with the oil and season with salt and pepper. Bake until crisp and golden brown, about 5 minutes.

2. **Sauté** the prosciutto in a large non-stick frying pan over medium heat until crisp and golden brown, about 5 minutes. Break into smaller pieces.

3. **Put** the lettuce in a salad bowl. Add the bread cubes, eggs, and Parmesan cheese. Top with the prosciutto and season generously with pepper.

4. **To prepare the dressing,** combine the oil, cream, and anchovies in a small bowl. Mix with a fork, mashing the anchovies until they dissolve into the oil and cream.

5. **Whisk** in the lemon juice, garlic, Worcestershire sauce, mustard, and vinegar.

6. **Drizzle** the dressing over the salad and serve immediately.

AMOUNT PER SERVING	575	22g	48g	1g	15g	2.4g
NUTRITION FACTS	CALORIES	PROTEIN	FAT	FIBER	CARBS	SALT
PERCENT DAILY VALUES (based on 2000 calories)	28%	48%	59%	4%	12%	44%

green pea salad

In spring and early summer, use fresh peas to make this nutritious salad.

Serves 6

10 minutes

15 minutes

5–10 minutes

1

SALAD

2 tablespoons extra-virgin olive oil

3 cups (450 g) frozen peas

½ large red bell pepper (capsicum), seeded and diced

1 large orange, segmented

DRESSING

⅓ cup (90 ml) extra-virgin olive oil

1 tablespoon finely chopped fresh mint

2 tablespoons freshly squeezed orange juice

1 tablespoon freshly squeezed lemon juice

Salt and freshly ground black pepper

1. **To prepare the salad,** heat the oil in a medium saucepan over medium heat. Add the peas and bell pepper and sauté until tender, 5–10 minutes. Set aside to cool a little, about 15 minutes.

2. **Put** the pea mixture in a salad bowl and stir in the orange segments.

3. **To prepare the dressing,** whisk the oil, mint, and orange and lemon juices in a small bowl. Season with salt and pepper.

4. **Drizzle** the dressing over the salad, toss well, and serve.

AMOUNT PER SERVING **NUTRITION FACTS** PERCENT DAILY VALUES (based on 2 000 calories)	239 CALORIES 11%	7g PROTEIN 15%	20g FAT 25%	6g FIBER 24%	8g CARBS 6%	0.2g SALT 4%

If you liked this recipe, you will love these as well.

warm fennel & asparagus **salad**

summer greens with lime & cilantro

italian salad

If pressed for time, use ready-to-serve marinated artichoke hearts and bell peppers. Both should be well drained.

Serves 6

30 minutes

15 minutes

2

4	fresh artichokes
¼	cup (60 ml) freshly squeezed lemon juice
2	large yellow bell peppers (capsicums), seeded and sliced
½	cup (125 ml) extra-virgin olive oil
1	teaspoon French mustard
6	salt-cured anchovy fillets

	Freshly ground black pepper
1	cup (50 g) mixed salad greens
1	fennel bulb, thinly sliced
6	sun-dried tomatoes in oil, drained and chopped
18	black olives
	Fresh basil leaves
	Parmesan cheese, in flakes

1. **To prepare the artichokes,** trim the stalk and cut off the top third of the leaves. Remove the tough outer leaves by bending them down and snapping them off at the base. Cut in half and use a sharp knife to remove any fuzzy choke. Slice thinly and place in a bowl of cold water with 2 tablespoons of the lemon juice. If liked, blanch the artichokes in boiling water for 1 minute. Drain well, and let cool a little.

2. **To prepare the bell peppers,** heat a broiler (grill) and broil the bell peppers until the skins are charred and blackened. Cook as briefly as possible so that the flesh remains firm. Put the charred peppers in a plastic bag and twist tightly shut. Leave until cool enough to handle, about 10 minutes. Gently remove the charred skins with your fingers. Cut into long thin pieces.

Do not rinse the bell peppers (this will remove some of the delicious flavor), but clean as much as possible with paper towels.

3. **To prepare the dressing,** whisk the remaining 2 tablespoons of lemon juice in a small bowl with the oil and mustard. Add the anchovies and whisk until dissolved in the oil. Season with pepper.

4. **Put** the salad greens in a bowl. Add a little of the dressing and toss lightly. Divide the salad greens evenly among six serving plates.

5. **Arrange** the fennel, artichokes, bell peppers, tomatoes, olives, and basil on the salad greens. Drizzle with the remaining dressing.

6. **Top** with the Parmesan and serve.

AMOUNT PER SERVING	334 CALORIES 16%	5g PROTEIN 11%	33g FAT 41%	2g FIBER 8%	6g CARBS 5%	1.9g SALT 34%
NUTRITION FACTS PERCENT DAILY VALUES (based on 2000 calories)						

arugula & pineapple salad

Keep the pineapple in the refrigerator until just before you prepare this refreshing summer salad.

 Serves 4

15 minutes

 1

1	pineapple, peeled, quartered, and cored
3	bunches arugula (rocket) leaves
1 ½	cups (150 g) snow pea (sugar pea or mangetout) shoots
¼	cup (60 ml) extra-virgin olive oil
	Salt and freshly ground black pepper

1. **Slice** the pineapple into bite-size pieces.

2. **Combine** the pineapple, arugula, and snow pea shoots in a large salad bowl.

3. **Drizzle** with the oil and toss gently. Season with salt and pepper. Serve at once.

AMOUNT PER SERVING NUTRITION FACTS PERCENT DAILY VALUES (based on 2000 calories)	CALORIES 183 9%	PROTEIN 3g 7%	FAT 14g 17%	FIBER 4g 16%	CARBS 13g 10%	SALT 0.2g 4%

If you liked this recipe, you will love these as well.

kiwi fruit & mushroom salad

30

arugula, corn & kiwi fruit salad

42

woodland salad with raspberries & wild rice

166

mozzarella & tomato salad

This classic Italian salad—known as *insalata caprese* in Italy—comes from the region around Naples in southern Italy, the home of fresh mozzarella cheese.

Serves 4

10 minutes

SALAD

4	medium ripe salad or beefsteak tomatoes, sliced
8	ounces (250 g) fresh mozzarella cheese, sliced
	Fresh basil leaves

DRESSING

½	cup (125 ml) extra-virgin olive oil
3	tablespoons red wine vinegar
	Salt

1

1. **To prepare the salad,** arrange the tomato slices and mozzarella on four individual serving plates. Garnish with the basil leaves.

2. **To prepare the dressing,** whisk the oil and vinegar in a small bowl. Season with salt.

3. **Drizzle** a little dressing over each salad and serve.

AMOUNT PER SERVING	431 CALORIES	12g PROTEIN	41g FAT	1g FIBER	3g CARBS	0.6g SALT
NUTRITION FACTS PERCENT DAILY VALUES (based on 2000 calories)	21%	26%	51%	4%	2%	11%

If you liked this recipe, you will love these as well.

pinzimonio

italian salad

50

56

panzanella with tomato vinaigrette

132

mushroom & spinach salad

Serve this light salad as an appetizer or as a side dish with baked fish.

Serves 4

15 minutes

1

2 cups (100 g) baby spinach leaves

8 ounces (250 g) button mushrooms, thinly sliced

3 tablespoons freshly squeezed lemon juice or balsamic vinegar

Salt and freshly ground black pepper

1/3 cup (90 ml) extra-virgin olive oil

2 ounces (60 g) Parmesan cheese, in shavings

1. **Arrange** the spinach on four individual serving plates.

2. **Put** the mushrooms in a bowl with the lemon juice or vinegar. Season with salt and pepper and toss lightly.

3. **Pile** the mushrooms on top of the spinach leaves.

4. **Drizzle** the salads with oil, top with the Parmesan, and serve.

AMOUNT PER SERVING	262	8g	25g	2g	2g	0.5g
NUTRITION FACTS	CALORIES	PROTEIN	FAT	FIBER	CARBS	SALT
PERCENT DAILY VALUES (based on 2000 calories)	13%	17%	31%	8%	2%	8%

If you liked this recipe, you will love this as well.

kiwi fruit & mushroom salad

30

marinated eggplant salad

This salad can be prepared ahead of time and stored in the refrigerator for up to 2–3 days. Take out of the refrigerator about 30 minutes before serving.

Serves 4

15 minutes

5 hours

15–20 minutes

 2

2	medium eggplant (aubergines), with skin, cut into ½-inch (1-cm) thick slices
1	tablespoon coarse sea salt
5	tablespoons (75 ml) extra-virgin olive oil
4	cloves garlic, thinly sliced
1	red bell pepper (capsicum), seeded and sliced

1	tablespoon finely chopped fresh parsley
1	cup (100 g) pitted black olives
½	cup (125 ml) white wine vinegar
½	cup (125 ml) water
1	teaspoon freshly ground black pepper
1	teaspoon cayenne pepper

1. **Place** a layer of eggplant in a colander and sprinkle with the coarse sea salt. Repeat, sprinkling each layer with salt. Let drain for 1 hour.

2. **Shake** the salt off the eggplant and dry the slices on paper towels.

3. **Heat** the oil in a large frying pan over medium heat. Fry the eggplant in batches until tender and lightly browned, about 5 minutes each batch. Drain on paper towels.

4. **Layer** the eggplant, garlic, bell pepper, parsley, and olives in a shallow glass or ceramic dish.

5. **Combine** the vinegar, water, and both types of pepper in a small saucepan over medium heat. Bring to a boil. Pour over the layered eggplant in the dish.

6. **Let cool** to room temperature. Cover the dish and chill in the refrigerator for at least 4 hours before serving.

AMOUNT PER SERVING	241	5g	21g	4g	7g	2.3g
NUTRITION FACTS	**CALORIES**	**PROTEIN**	**FAT**	**FIBER**	**CARBS**	**SALT**
PERCENT DAILY VALUES (based on 2 000 calories)	12%	11%	26%	16%	5%	41%

If you liked this recipe, you will love these as well.

couscous salad with eggplant

124

eggplant salad with prosciutto

258

roasted beets with balsamic vinegar

If desired, serve this salad with a bowl of sour cream or plain yogurt.

Serves 6

15 minutes

30–45 minutes

2

18	small beets (beetroots), with peel, green stems attached if possible
3	tablespoons extra-virgin olive oil
	Salt and freshly ground black pepper
2	tablespoons butter
2	tablespoons balsamic vinegar
3	tablespoons fresh dill, snipped
½	cup (70 g) hazelnuts, roasted and chopped

1. If the beets have their greens attached, remove them and set aside.

2. Preheat the oven to 400°F (200°C/gas 6).

3. Put the beets in a large bowl and drizzle with the oil. Toss well. Transfer the beets to a baking dish. Cover with foil or a lid and roast for 30–45 minutes (depending on size) until tender.

4. Remove the beets from the oven and set aside until cool enough to handle. Peel the skin away and discard. Slice the beets lengthwise and season with salt and pepper.

5. Heat 1 tablespoon of butter in a large frying pan over medium-high heat. Add the beet greens and toss until wilted, 1–2 minutes. Remove and set aside.

6. Add the balsamic vinegar to the pan and bring to a boil. Whisk in the remaining butter. Add the beets to the pan and toss until the balsamic vinegar mixture has reduced and the beets are covered in a shiny sheen.

7. Transfer the beets to a bowl and top with the wilted greens. Sprinkle with the dill and roasted hazelnuts. Season with extra pepper if desired, and serve.

AMOUNT PER SERVING	197	3g	17g	2g	8g	0.2g
NUTRITION FACTS	CALORIES	PROTEIN	FAT	FIBER	CARBS	SALT
PERCENT DAILY VALUES (based on 2000 calories)	9%	7%	21%	8%	6%	4%

If you liked this recipe, you will love these as well.

roasted beets with orange & fennel

68

moroccan vegetable salad

180

roasted beets with orange & fennel

Serve this eye-catching salad as an appetizer.

Serves 6

35 minutes

1 hour

1

SALAD

1	tablespoon brown sugar
1	teaspoon salt
2	tablespoons finely chopped fresh rosemary
3	tablespoons extra-virgin olive oil
6	large beets (beetroots), trimmed but with peel
1	bulb fennel, thinly sliced
3	oranges, peeled and divided into segments
¾	cup (150 g) toasted hazelnuts, chopped

DILL VINAIGRETTE

½	cup (25 g) finely chopped fresh dill
3	tablespoons balsamic vinegar
½	cup (125 ml) extra-virgin olive oil
	Salt and freshly ground black pepper

1. **Preheat** the oven to 350°F (180°C/gas 4).

2. **To prepare the salad,** combine the brown sugar, salt, rosemary, and oil in a large bowl. Whisk until well blended.

3. **Add** the whole beets and toss in the oil mixture, making sure that the skins are well-coated and shiny with oil. Wrap each beet in aluminum foil and place in a baking dish. Roast for about 1 hour, until just tender.

4. **Set aside** until cool enough to handle. Peel off the skins with your fingers and a knife. Cut the beets into thick slices. Put in a shallow salad bowl and top with the oranges and fennel.

5. **To prepare the dill vinaigrette,** whisk the dill, balsamic vinegar, and oil in a small bowl. Season with salt and pepper and whisk again.

6. **Drizzle** the vinaigrette over the salad. Sprinkle with the hazelnuts and serve.

AMOUNT PER SERVING	435	5g	41g	4g	13g	0.9g
NUTRITION FACTS	CALORIES	PROTEIN	FAT	FIBER	CARBS	SALT
PERCENT DAILY VALUES (based on 2 000 calories)	21%	11%	51%	16%	10%	17%

If you liked this recipe, you will love this as well.

roasted beets with balsamic vinegar

66

lettuce & grapefruit salad

This light salad is brimming with vitamin C. Serve as an appetizer or to accompany grilled meats.

Serves 4

15 minutes

1

SALAD

1	romaine (cos) lettuce, torn
1	large grapefruit, peeled and divided into segments
1	small sweet red onion, diced
1/2	small red cabbage, shredded
	Thin strips of orange zest, to garnish (optional)

VINAIGRETTE

1/3	cup (90 ml) extra-virgin olive oil
3	tablespoons freshly squeezed orange juice
2	tablespoons freshly squeezed lemon juice
	Salt and freshly ground black pepper

1. **To prepare the salad,** put the lettuce in a salad bowl. Add the grapefruit, onion, and cabbage and toss well.

2. **To prepare the vinaigrette,** whisk the oil, orange juice, lemon juice, salt, and pepper in a small bowl.

3. **Drizzle** the vinaigrette over the salad and toss lightly. Serve at once, garnished with the strips of orange zest, if desired.

AMOUNT PER SERVING	217	2g	21g	2g	7g	0.2g
NUTRITION FACTS	**CALORIES**	**PROTEIN**	**FAT**	**FIBER**	**CARBS**	**SALT**
PERCENT DAILY VALUES (based on 2000 calories)	10%	4%	26%	8%	5%	4%

If you liked this recipe, you will love these as well.

pink grapefruit & quinoa salad

130

new mexican chicken salad

246

spring salad

If desired, replace the ready-to-serve marinated artichokes with 4 fresh artichoke hearts. See page 56 for instructions on how to clean the fresh artichokes.

Serves 6

20 minutes

1–2 minutes

1

SALAD

1 head frisée (curly endive), torn

1 head red radicchio, leaves separated

12 thin, tender asparagus spears, trimmed and cut into short lengths

12 marinated artichoke hearts, halved

4 carrots, cut into thin strips

3 hard-boiled eggs, sliced

VINAIGRETTE

½ cup (125 ml) extra-virgin olive oil

¼ cup (60 ml) white wine vinegar

Salt

2 tablespoons capers, drained

1. **To prepare the salad,** combine the frisée and radicchio leaves in a shallow salad bowl.

2. **Blanch** the asparagus in lightly salted boiling water for 1–2 minutes. Refresh under cold water and drain thoroughly.

3. **Arrange** the asparagus, artichokes, carrots, and eggs on the salad greens.

4. **To prepare the vinaigrette,** whisk the oil, vinegar, and salt in a bowl and stir in the capers. Drizzle over the salad, toss well, and serve.

AMOUNT PER SERVING	278	10g	23g	4g	8g	0.2g
NUTRITION FACTS	CALORIES	PROTEIN	FAT	FIBER	CARBS	SALT
PERCENT DAILY VALUES (based on 2 000 calories)	13%	22%	28%	16%	6%	4%

If you liked this recipe, you will love these as well.

green pea salad

54

spring chicken salad

248

watermelon salad

Serve this light and refreshing salad as an appetizer on hot summer days or with roasted fish or meats throughout the year.

 Serves 6

 10 minutes

2	hearts romaine (cos) lettuce, torn
2	cups (400 g) peeled and cubed watermelon
⅓	cup (90 ml) extra-virgin olive oil
¼	cup (60 ml) red wine vinegar
	Salt
	Cracked pepper

 1

1. **Put** the lettuce a medium salad bowl. Add the watermelon.

2. **Whisk** the oil and vinegar in a small bowl until well mixed. Season with salt and whisk again.

3. **Drizzle** the dressing over the salad and toss well. Season with cracked pepper and serve.

AMOUNT PER SERVING	149	1g	14g	1g	5g	0.2g
NUTRITION FACTS	**CALORIES**	**PROTEIN**	**FAT**	**FIBER**	**CARBS**	**SALT**
PERCENT DAILY VALUES (based on 2 000 calories)	7%	2%	17%	4%	4%	4%

If you liked this recipe, you will love these as well.

melon, zucchini & pancetta **salad**

28

arugula & pineapple **salad**

58

summer greens with lime & cilantro

Replace the cilantro with parsley or mint, if preferred.

 Serves 6

 15 minutes

 5 minutes

 1

SALAD

8	ounces (250 g) snow peas (mangetout)
1	bunch thin, tender asparagus spears
8	ounces (250 g) sugar snap peas
2	cups (250 g) fresh peas
4	ounces (125 g) cherry tomatoes, cut in half

DRESSING

½	cup (125 ml) extra-virgin olive oil
2	tablespoons freshly squeezed lime juice
1	tablespoon white wine vinegar
	Salt
3	tablespoons finely chopped fresh cilantro (coriander)

1. **To prepare the salad,** blanch the snow peas, asparagus, and sugar snap peas in salted boiling water for 1–2 minutes. Drain and refresh in a bowl of iced cold water. Drain again thoroughly.

2. **Cook** the fresh peas in salted boiling water until tender, 2–3 minutes. Drain and refresh in iced water. Drain again thoroughly.

3. **Combine** all the vegetables with the cherry tomatoes in a salad bowl.

4. **To prepare the dressing,** whisk the oil, lime juice, vinegar, salt, and cilantro in a small bowl.

5. **Drizzle** over the salad vegetables and serve.

AMOUNT PER SERVING	244 CALORIES	7g PROTEIN	20g FAT	8g FIBER	10g CARBS	0.2g SALT
NUTRITION FACTS PERCENT DAILY VALUES (based on 2 000 calories)	12%	15%	25%	32%	8%	4%

If you liked this recipe, you will love these as well.

arugula, corn & kiwi fruit salad

42

lettuce & grapefruit salad

70

warm salad with bell peppers & rosemary

Low in calories, bell peppers are packed with nutrients, including vitamin C, beta-carotene, vitamin K, thiamine, and folic acid. Eating bell peppers regularly is believed to lower the risk of blood clots forming and reduce the risk of heart attacks and strokes.

Serves 4

10 minutes

15 minutes

25–30 minutes

2

2	tablespoons extra-virgin olive oil
1	large red onion, thickly sliced
3	tablespoons finely chopped fresh rosemary
3	cloves garlic, finely chopped
6	large peppers (capsicums), assorted colors, seeded and cut into long thin strips
1	tablespoon balsamic vinegar Salt and freshly ground black pepper

1. **Heat** the oil in a large frying pan over medium heat. Add the onion and rosemary and sauté until softened, about 3 minutes.

2. **Add** the garlic and bell peppers and simmer in the rosemary-flavored oil over low heat until the bell peppers are tender, 15–20 minutes.

3. **Add** the balsamic vinegar and simmer for 5 minutes. Remove from the heat and let cool for 15 minutes.

4. **Season** with salt and pepper and serve warm.

| AMOUNT PER SERVING **NUTRITION FACTS** PERCENT DAILY VALUES (based on 2 000 calories) | 143 CALORIES 7% | 3g PROTEIN 7% | 7g FAT 9% | 5g FIBER 20% | 19g CARBS 15% | 0.2g SALT 4% |

If you liked this recipe, you will love these as well.

warm bean salad with prosciutto

110

warm steak salad with papaya & onion

272

watercress & pear salad

Watercress has a pungent, slightly peppery taste that works well in salads. Here its flavor is offset by the sweet pears and the salty Parmesan.

 Serves 6

 15 minutes

 1

SALAD

2   bunches watercress, tough stems discarded

2   ripe pears, cored and thinly sliced

2   ounces (60 g) Parmesan cheese, in shavings

DRESSING

½   cup (125 ml) extra-virgin olive oil

2   tablespoons freshly squeezed lemon juice

Salt and freshly ground black pepper

1. **To prepare the salad,** put the watercress in a bowl and top with the pears.

2. **To prepare the dressing,** whisk the oil, lemon juice, and salt in a small bowl.

3. **Drizzle** the salad with the dressing and toss gently. Top with the Parmesan, season with pepper, and serve.

AMOUNT PER SERVING **NUTRITION FACTS** PERCENT DAILY VALUES (based on 2 000 calories)	233 CALORIES 11%	5g PROTEIN 11%	22g FAT 27%	1g FIBER 4%	5g CARBS 4%	0.2g SALT 4%

If you liked this recipe, you will love these as well.

cheese, pear & kiwi fruit salad

26

rice salad with apple & walnuts

164

Hearty &
Wholesome

bean salad with artichokes

Cannellini beans are a delicious Italian bean with a mild, nutty flavor and a lovely creamy texture. They are excellent for salads as well as in soups and purées.

 Serves 4

 10 minutes

 15 minutes

 1–2 minutes

 1

SALAD

14	ounces (400 g) green beans, trimmed
1	red bell pepper (capsicum), cut into thin strips
1	(14-ounce/400-g) can cannellini beans, rinsed and drained
6	canned artichoke hearts, drained and halved

DRESSING

⅓	cup (90 ml) extra-virgin olive oil
2	tablespoons red wine vinegar
	Salt and freshly ground black pepper

1. **To prepare the salad,** blanch the green beans in salted boiling water for 1–2 minutes. Drain well and refresh in iced water. Drain again thoroughly.

2. **Put** the bell pepper in a medium bowl of iced water for 15 minutes then drain.

3. **Combine** the green beans, cannellini beans, artichokes, and bell pepper in a salad bowl.

4. **To prepare the dressing,** whisk the oil, vinegar, salt, and pepper in a small bowl. Drizzle over the salad, toss gently, and serve.

AMOUNT PER SERVING **NUTRITION FACTS** PERCENT DAILY VALUES (based on 2000 calories)	295 CALORIES 14%	9g PROTEIN 20%	21g FAT 26%	7g FIBER 28%	19g CARBS 15%	0.1g SALT 1%

If you liked this recipe, you will love these as well.

middle eastern bean & artichoke salad

100

warm bean salad with prosciutto

110

mixed turkey salad with vegetables

254

two bean salad

This salad can be prepared a day or two before serving; it will only gain in flavor if covered and kept well chilled. Butter beans are also known as lima beans.

Serves 4

15 minutes

2 hours

2 minutes

1

SALAD

8	ounces (250 g) green beans, topped and tailed
1	cup (200 g) canned butter beans or lima beans, drained
½	cucumber, thinly sliced
½	red bell pepper (capsicum), cut into thin strips
½	red onion, halved and sliced
4	ripe tomatoes, diced
2	tablespoons finely chopped fresh basil

DRESSING

⅓	cup (90 ml) extra-virgin olive oil
2	tablespoons white wine vinegar
	Salt and freshly ground black pepper

1. **To prepare the salad,** blanch the green beans in lightly salted boiling water for 2 minutes. Drain and refresh in iced water. Drain again thoroughly.

2. **Combine** the green beans, butter beans, cucumber, bell pepper, onion, tomatoes, and basil in a salad bowl.

3. **To prepare the dressing,** whisk the oil, vinegar, salt, and pepper in a small bowl.

4. **Drizzle** the dressing over the salad and toss well. Cover and chill in the refrigerator for at least 2 hours before serving.

AMOUNT PER SERVING	274	6g	21g	5g	16g	0.2g
NUTRITION FACTS	**CALORIES**	**PROTEIN**	**FAT**	**FIBER**	**CARBS**	**SALT**
PERCENT DAILY VALUES (based on 2 000 calories)	13%	13%	26%	20%	12%	4%

If you liked this recipe, you will love these as well.

bean salad with artichokes

84

marinated bean salad

98

mixed beans with tuna

192

garbanzo bean salad
with tzatziki dressing

Garbanzo beans are full of natural goodness and the light yogurt dressing in this recipe really enhances their distinctive flavor.

Serves 6

15 minutes

1

SALAD

2   (14-ounce/400-g) cans garbanzo beans (chickpeas), drained
2   firm, ripe tomatoes, diced
1   green bell pepper (capsicum), cut into thin strips
1   yellow bell pepper (capsicum), cut into thin strips

TZATZIKI DRESSING

¼   cup (60 ml) extra-virgin olive oil
2   tablespoons cider vinegar
½   cup (125 ml) low-fat yogurt
1   tablespoon Dijon mustard
1   clove garlic, finely chopped
1   teaspoon sugar
    Salt and freshly ground black pepper

1. **To prepare the salad,** combine the garbanzo beans, tomatoes, and bell peppers in a bowl.

2. **To prepare the tzatziki dressing,** whisk the oil, vinegar, yogurt, mustard, garlic, sugar, salt, and pepper in a small bowl.

3. **Drizzle** the dressing over the salad and toss gently.

4. **Divide** the salad evenly among six individual salad bowls and serve.

AMOUNT PER SERVING	168	5g	11g	3g	14g	0.3g
NUTRITION FACTS	CALORIES	PROTEIN	FAT	FIBER	CARBS	SALT
PERCENT DAILY VALUES (based on 2 000 calories)	8%	11%	14%	12%	11%	5%

If you liked this recipe, you will love these as well.

middle eastern bean & artichoke salad

100

greek orzo salad with olives & pepper

138

grilled bell pepper pasta salad

154

chunky lentil salad

Lentils are rich in protein and carbohydrates and are a good source of calcium, phosphorus, iron, and B vitamins. Whole lentils don't require soaking and will cook in about 30 minutes.

 Serves 4

10 minutes

1 hour

30 minutes

1

SALAD

1   cup (200 g) red lentils

3   tomatoes, chopped

3   tablespoons finely chopped fresh parsley

DRESSING

5   tablespoons extra-virgin olive oil

2   tablespoons red wine or balsamic vinegar

1   clove garlic, finely chopped

Salt

1. **To prepare the salad**, cook the lentils in lightly salted boiling water until tender, about 30 minutes.

2. **Drain** the lentils through a sieve lined with a clean kitchen towel. Squeeze out as much moisture as possible, then put in a medium bowl. Stir in the tomatoes and parsley.

3. **To prepare the dressing**, whisk the oil, vinegar, garlic, and salt in a small bowl. Add the dressing to the lentil and tomato salad and toss gently.

4. **Cover** and set aside for at least 1 hour at room temperature.

AMOUNT PER SERVING	295	12g	15g	6g	30g	0.1g
NUTRITION FACTS	**CALORIES**	**PROTEIN**	**FAT**	**FIBER**	**CARBS**	**SALT**
PERCENT DAILY VALUES (based on 2 000 calories)	14%	26%	19%	24%	23%	2%

If you liked this recipe, you will love these as well.

lentil & radish salad

94

roasted corn & bean salad

102

quinoa, corn & pinto bean salad

128

spicy garbanzo bean salad
with vegetables

Garam masala is a blend of spices used in northern Indian cooking. *Garam* comes from Persian and means "hot," while *masala* comes originally from Arabic and means "spices or seasonings." Garam masala is widely available in Asian food stores.

Serves 8

2 hours

12 hours

2 hours

3

1¼	cups (200 g) garbanzo beans (chickpeas)
4	onions, halved
1	teaspoon whole cloves
4	bay leaves
¼	cup (60 ml) peanut oil
4	cloves garlic, finely chopped
1	teaspoon ground turmeric
2	teaspoons ground cumin
2	teaspoons garam masala

1	cup (250 ml) water
3	tablespoons tomato paste (concentrate)
2	red bell peppers (capsicum), diced
4	zucchini (courgettes), thinly sliced on the diagonal
	Salt and freshly ground black pepper
1	pound (500 g) baby spinach

1. **Soak** the garbanzo beans in cold water for 12 hours or overnight. Drain.

2. **Combine** the garbanzo beans, 2 halved onions, cloves, and bay leaves in a large saucepan and cover with cold water. Bring to a boil and simmer until the garbanzo beans are tender, about 2 hours.

3. **Drain** the garbanzo beans, discarding the onions, cloves, and bay leaves.

4. **Slice** the remaining 2 onions. Heat the oil in a medium saucepan over medium heat and sauté the garlic and onions for 3 minutes. Add the turmeric, cumin, and garam masala and sauté for 1 minute.

5. **Add** the garbanzo beans, water, tomato paste, and bell peppers. Simmer for 10 minutes. Add the zucchini and season with salt and pepper. Stir well, then remove from the heat.

6. **Let cool,** then add the spinach. Toss well before serving.

AMOUNT PER SERVING	210	10g	10g	4g	23g	0.3g
NUTRITION FACTS	**CALORIES**	**PROTEIN**	**FAT**	**FIBER**	**CARBS**	**SALT**
PERCENT DAILY VALUES (based on 2 000 calories)	10%	22%	12%	16%	18%	5%

If you liked this recipe, you will love these as well.

thai **noodle** salad

136

thai **fish & mango** salad

218

spiced chicken & dhal salad

238

lentil & radish salad

Radishes are best known for their distinctive peppery taste and are great for spicing up salads. If the radishes have leaves, be careful in preparing them as they can cause skin irritation.

 Serves 6

 15 minutes

 30 minutes

 30 minutes

 1

SALAD
1¼	cups (250 g) red lentils
1	onion, chopped
1	carrot, chopped
4	tablespoons finely chopped fresh parsley
1	clove garlic, finely chopped
½	teaspoon dried thyme
1	bay leaf
	Salt and freshly ground black pepper
12	fresh radishes, thinly sliced
2	tablespoons snipped fresh chives

LEMON VINAIGRETTE
½	cup (125 ml) extra-virgin olive oil
2	tablespoons freshly squeezed lemon juice
	Salt and freshly ground black pepper

1. **To prepare the salad**, combine the lentils, onion, carrot, 1 tablespoon of parsley, garlic, thyme, and bay leaf in a saucepan and cover with water.

2. **Bring** to a boil, then simmer until the lentils are tender, about 30 minutes. Drain, discard the bay leaf, and transfer the mixture to a large bowl.

3. **Season** with salt and pepper. Let cool for 30 minutes.

4. **Add** the radishes, chives, and remaining parsley.

5. **To prepare the lemon vinaigrette**, whisk the oil, lemon juice, salt, and pepper in a small bowl.

6. **Drizzle** the vinaigrette over the salad, toss well, and serve.

AMOUNT PER SERVING	477	16g	29g	8g	40g	0.1g
NUTRITION FACTS	**CALORIES**	**PROTEIN**	**FAT**	**FIBER**	**CARBS**	**SALT**
PERCENT DAILY VALUES (based on 2 000 calories)	23%	35%	36%	32%	31%	1%

If you liked this recipe, you will love these as well.

chunky lentil salad

90

crunchy lentil salad

96

salmon & lentil salad

212

crunchy lentil salad

Bean sprouts of all kinds are highly nutritious. Low in calories, they are rich in vitamins, minerals, amino acids, protein, and beneficial enzymes and phytochemicals.

Serves 4

10 minutes

2 hours

30 minutes

2

1	cup (200 g) brown lentils
1 ½	cups (100 g) crunchy fresh small bean sprouts or alfalfa sprouts
2	tablespoons coarsely chopped fresh mint
½	red onion, finely chopped
½	cup (125 ml) freshly squeezed orange juice
2	tablespoons extra-virgin olive oil
1	tablespoon balsamic or red wine vinegar
1	teaspoon finely grated orange zest
1	teaspoon ground cumin
	Salt and freshly ground black pepper

1. **Put** the lentils in a saucepan of lightly salted water and bring to a boil. Simmer until tender, about 30 minutes. Drain and rinse under cold running water. Drain again and dry on a clean kitchen towel.

2. **Transfer** the lentils to a salad bowl and add all the remaining ingredients. Toss well to combine. Cover and chill in the refrigerator for 2 hours before serving.

AMOUNT PER SERVING	218 CALORIES	13g PROTEIN	7g FAT	5g FIBER	28g CARBS	0.1g SALT
NUTRITION FACTS PERCENT DAILY VALUES (based on 2000 calories)	10%	28%	9%	20%	22%	2%

If you liked this recipe, you will love these as well.

lentil & radish salad

94

roasted corn & bean salad

102

marinated bean salad

This is a perfect party appetizer since it can be prepared in advance. Serve with lots of warm, freshly baked bread.

 Serves 4

15 minutes

4–6 hours

2–3 minutes

1

SALAD

4 ounces (100 g) green beans, halved

2 small zucchini (courgettes), cut into matchsticks

1 small carrot, cut into matchsticks

1 cup (250 g) canned red kidney beans, drained and rinsed

1 cup (250 g) canned garbanzo beans (chickpeas), drained and rinsed

1 cup (200 g) canned butter beans or lima beans, drained and rinsed

1 small red pepper (capsicum), cut into strips

2 tablespoons finely chopped fresh parsley

2 tablespoons finely chopped fresh basil

DRESSING

1/3 cup (90 ml) extra-virgin olive oil

2 tablespoons red wine vinegar

1 clove garlic, finely chopped
Salt and freshly ground black pepper

1. **To prepare the salad,** steam the green beans, zucchini, and carrot until just tender, 2–3 minutes. Drain and refresh under cold running water.

2. **Combine** the cooked vegetables, red kidney beans, garbanzo beans, butter beans, bell pepper, parsley, and basil in a large salad bowl.

3. **To prepare the dressing,** whisk the oil, vinegar, garlic, salt, and pepper in a small bowl.

4. **Drizzle** the dressing over the salad and toss well. Cover and refrigerate for 4–6 hours. Toss again just before serving.

AMOUNT PER SERVING	453	14g	29g	12g	35g	1.6g
NUTRITION FACTS	**CALORIES**	**PROTEIN**	**FAT**	**FIBER**	**CARBS**	**SALT**
PERCENT DAILY VALUES (based on 2000 calories)	22%	30%	36%	48%	27%	26%

If you liked this recipe, you will love these as well.

spicy bean & vegetable salad

104

trattoria bean salad

108

middle eastern bean & artichoke salad

Full of the exotic flavors of the Middle East, this salad is a quick and tasty treat.

 Serves 6

10 minutes

5 minutes

1

SALAD

1¼	pounds (600 g) green beans
2	(14-ounce/400-g) cans garbanzo beans (chickpeas), drained and rinsed
8	marinated, ready-to-eat artichoke hearts, quartered
1	small red onion, finely sliced
1	medium carrot, grated
½	cup (25 g) finely chopped fresh parsley
½	cup (25 g) finely chopped fresh cilantro (coriander)
2	tablespoons finely chopped fresh dill
¾	cup (90 g) hazelnuts, toasted and coarsely chopped

DRESSING

½	cup (125 ml) extra-virgin olive oil
	Freshly squeezed juice of 1 large lemon
2	tablespoons white wine vinegar
1	clove garlic, finely chopped
1	teaspoon Dijon mustard
1	teaspoon ground cumin
	Salt and freshly ground black pepper

1. **To prepare the salad,** steam the green beans until crunchy tender, 2–3 minutes. Drain well and refresh in cold water.

2. **Put** the green beans in a large salad bowl and add the garbanzo beans, artichokes, onion, carrot, parsley, cilantro, and dill. Toss well.

3. **To prepare the dressing,** whisk the oil, lemon juice, vinegar, garlic, mustard, cumin, salt, and pepper in a small bowl.

4. **Drizzle** the dressing over the salad and toss well. Top with the hazelnuts and serve.

AMOUNT PER SERVING	363 CALORIES	10g PROTEIN	31g FAT	6g FIBER	15g CARBS	0.3g SALT
NUTRITION FACTS PERCENT DAILY VALUES (based on 2000 calories)	17%	22%	38%	24%	12%	5%

If you liked this recipe, you will love these as well.

garbanzo bean salad with tzatziki dressing

88

spicy garbanzo bean salad with vegetables

92

roasted corn & bean salad

If fresh corn is out of season, replace with 1 small can of corn, well drained.

 Serves 6

15 minutes

15–20 minutes

 2

4	ears fresh corn (sweet corn)
2	red bell peppers (capsicums), seeded and chopped
1	green bell pepper (capsicum), seeded and chopped
1	red onion, finely chopped
1	tablespoon hot paprika
1	tablespoon ground cumin
3	tablespoons extra-virgin olive oil
2	cloves garlic, finely chopped
6	baby yellow summer squash, chopped

2	cups (400 g) canned lima beans, drained and rinsed
2	cups (400 g) canned red kidney beans, drained and rinsed
½	cup (125 ml) vegetable stock
1	teaspoon Tabasco sauce
1	teaspoon sugar
	Freshly squeezed juice of 2 limes
3	tablespoons finely chopped fresh cilantro (coriander)
	Salt and freshly ground black pepper

1. **Cut** the kernels from the corn cobs.

2. **Combine** the bell peppers, onion, paprika, cumin, and corn in a large nonstick frying pan and sauté over high heat until the vegetables begin to blister, 5–10 minutes. Transfer to a large bowl and set aside.

3. **Add** the oil, garlic, and squash to the frying pan and sauté for 5 minutes.

4. **Add** the lima beans, kidney beans, stock, Tabasco, and sugar. Cook over medium heat until the liquid has evaporated, about 5 minutes.

5. **Remove** from the heat and add the lime juice and cilantro. Season with salt and pepper.

6. **Add** the corn mixture and toss well. Serve warm or at room temperature.

AMOUNT PER SERVING	165	9g	2g	8g	31g	1.4g
NUTRITION FACTS	CALORIES	PROTEIN	FAT	FIBER	CARBS	SALT
PERCENT DAILY VALUES (based on 2000 calories)	8%	20%	2%	32%	24%	23%

If you liked this recipe, you will love these as well.

two bean salad

86

mixed beans with tuna

192

chicken, bean & arugula salad

234

spicy bean & vegetable salad

Cherry pepper, or pimiento, is a red, heart-shaped variety of pepper. It is sweet and succulent. Like bell peppers, it can be slivered and added raw to salads, or left whole and stuffed and baked as a side dish or starter.

Serves 2

10 minutes

1

SALAD

2 cups (400 g) canned butter beans or lima beans, drained and rinsed

2 zucchini (courgettes), thinly sliced lengthwise

2 fresh cherry peppers or 1 red bell pepper (capsicum), seeded and cut into strips
Fresh dill leaves, to garnish

DRESSING

¼ cup (60 ml) extra-virgin olive oil

1 tablespoon freshly squeezed lemon juice
Salt and freshly ground black pepper
Tabasco sauce

1. **To prepare the salad,** place the butter beans, zucchini, and pepper in a salad bowl.

2. **To prepare the dressing,** whisk the oil lemon juice, salt, black pepper, and Tabasco in a small bowl.

3. **Drizzle** the dressing over the salad and toss lightly. Garnish with the dill and serve.

AMOUNT PER SERVING	362	9g	28g	7g	19g	1.3g
NUTRITION FACTS	CALORIES	PROTEIN	FAT	FIBER	CARBS	SALT
PERCENT DAILY VALUES (based on 2 000 calories)	17%	20%	35%	28%	15%	22%

If you liked this recipe, you will love these as well.

trattoria bean salad

108

fennel sausage with zucchini

264

mixed salad with sun-dried tomato pesto

Large and juicy blue-black Kalamata olives are native to Greece. They are usually slit open before being packed in an olive oil or vinegar marinade. They are exported all over the world.

Serves 4

30 minutes

30 minutes

1

SUN-DRIED TOMATO PESTO

12   sun-dried tomatoes, drained
⅓   cup (90 ml) rice vinegar
1   tablespoon extra-virgin olive oil
2   teaspoons molasses
1   tablespoon soy sauce

SALAD

2   cups (100 g) baby arugula (rocket) leaves
1   bunch watercress

8   plum tomatoes, diced
6   scallions (spring onions), sliced
1   cup (100 g) Kalamata olives, pitted
2   cups (400 g) canned cannellini beans, drained and rinsed
  Salt and freshly ground black pepper
1   cup (120 g) coarsely chopped toasted walnuts

1. **To prepare the sun-dried tomato pesto,** put the sun-dried tomatoes in a medium bowl and add 1 cup (250 ml) of boiling water. Let stand until the water cools, about 30 minutes.

2. **Drain** and place in a food processor with the rice vinegar, oil, molasses, and soy sauce and chop until smooth.

3. **To prepare the salad,** combine the arugula and watercress in a large salad bowl and add the tomatoes, scallions, olives, and cannellini beans. Season with salt and pepper and toss gently.

4. **Drizzle** the salad with the sun-dried tomato pesto and toss well. Sprinkle with the walnuts and serve.

AMOUNT PER SERVING	633	13g	55g	7g	21g	3.1g
NUTRITION FACTS	CALORIES	PROTEIN	FAT	FIBER	CARBS	SALT
PERCENT DAILY VALUES (based on 2000 calories)	30%	28%	68%	28%	16%	52%

If you liked this recipe, you will love these as well.

italian salad

56

bread salad with poached trout

196

trattoria bean salad

Prosciutto, or *prosciutto crudo,* as it is known in Italy, is salted and air-dried ham. There are many types—Parma ham is probably the best known and is relatively sweet. If you get a chance, do try the saltier, more flavorful Tuscan variety.

 Serves 4

 10 minutes

 1

1	(14-ounce/400-g) can cannellini beans, drained and rinsed
1	stalk celery, thinly sliced
2	cloves garlic, finely chopped
2	tablespoons finely chopped fresh sage
1	tablespoon finely chopped fresh thyme
¼	cup (60 ml) extra-virgin olive oil
2	tablespoons freshly squeezed lemon juice
	Salt and freshly ground black pepper
12	slices prosciutto, chopped
	Freshly baked bread, to serve (optional)
½	cup (125 g) cream cheese (optional)

1. **Put** the cannellini beans in a large salad bowl. Add the celery, garlic, sage, thyme, oil, and lemon juice. Season lightly with salt and pepper.

2. **Add** the prosciutto and toss gently.

3. **Serve** with the bread and cream cheese.

AMOUNT PER SERVING	450	21g	36g	4g	12g	2.9g
NUTRITION FACTS	CALORIES	PROTEIN	FAT	FIBER	CARBS	SALT
PERCENT DAILY VALUES (based on 2000 calories)	22%	46%	44%	16%	9%	48%

If you liked this recipe, you will love these as well.

bean salad with artichokes

84

spicy bean & vegetable salad

104

warm bean salad
with prosciutto

Red radicchio is a variety of chicory that is native to Italy. It ranges in color from pink to deep red. It is widely available, but if you can't find it, substitute with crisp leaves from the inner heart of a fresh lettuce.

Serves 4

15 minutes

5–10 minutes

1

SALAD

16 red radicchio leaves

2 pounds (1 kg) fava (broad) beans in the pod, hulled, or 12 ounces (350 g) frozen fava (broad) beans

1 small red onion, finely chopped

4 large thin slices prosciutto, cut into thin strips

2 tablespoons finely chopped fresh parsley

Salt and freshly ground black pepper

RICH SOY DRESSING

⅓ cup (90 ml) extra-virgin olive oil

1½ tablespoons red wine vinegar

1 tablespoon freshly squeezed lemon juice

1½ tablespoons light soy sauce

Pinch of sugar

1. **To prepare the salad,** line a serving plate with the radicchio leaves.

2. **Cook** the beans in lightly salted water until tender, 5–10 minutes. Drain well.

3. **Put** the beans in a large bowl and add the onion, prosciutto, and parsley. Season with salt and pepper.

4. **To prepare the rich soy dressing,** whisk the oil, vinegar, lemon juice, soy sauce, and sugar in a small bowl.

5. **Drizzle** the dressing over the bean salad and toss well. Spoon onto the plate lined with radicchio and serve.

AMOUNT PER SERVING	324	14g	24g	6g	13g	2g
NUTRITION FACTS	**CALORIES**	**PROTEIN**	**FAT**	**FIBER**	**CARBS**	**SALT**
PERCENT DAILY VALUES (based on 2 000 calories)	16%	30%	30%	24%	10%	33%

If you liked this recipe, you will love these as well.

pear, roquefort & radicchio **salad**

32

wild salad greens with pancetta & balsamic vinegar

44

tabbouleh

This famous Middle Eastern salad can be served with pita bread as a starter or to accompany grilled meats. If desired, add 2–3 finely chopped scallions (spring onions).

 Serves 6

 20 minutes

 3 hours

 1

DRESSING

⅓	cup (90 ml) extra-virgin olive oil
3	tablespoons freshly squeezed lemon juice
2	cloves garlic, halved
	Salt

SALAD

1	cup (150 g) fine or medium bulgur
1	small cucumber, diced
2	tomatoes, diced
2	tablespoons finely chopped fresh mint
1	large bunch fresh parsley, very finely chopped

1. **To prepare the dressing,** combine the oil, lemon juice, garlic, and salt in a tightly closed screwtop jar. Set aside.

2. **To prepare the salad,** put the bulgur in a medium bowl and add plenty of cold water to cover. Set aside for 1 hour.

3. **Drain** the bulgur in a colander lined with a clean kitchen towel. Scoop the bulgur up in the towel and squeeze out all the excess moisture.

4. **Transfer** the bulgur to a salad bowl and add the cucumber, tomatoes, mint, and parsley. Toss well.

5. **Shake** the dressing in the jar, discard the garlic, and drizzle over the salad. Toss well.

6. **Cover** the salad and chill in the refrigerator for at least 2 hours before serving.

AMOUNT PER SERVING	218	3g	14g	5g	20g	0.2g
NUTRITION FACTS	CALORIES	PROTEIN	FAT	FIBER	CARBS	SALT
PERCENT DAILY VALUES (based on 2000 calories)	10%	7%	17%	20%	15%	4%

If you liked this recipe, you will love these as well.

bulgur salad

116

tuna barley salad

118

lamb & orange couscous salad

274

minted barley salad

Barley has a pleasant nutty flavor and a satisfyingly chewy texture. Pearl barley takes 25–30 minutes to cook, but quick-cooking varieties are now widely available; these will cook in about 10 minutes.

Serves 4

10 minutes

30 minutes

25–30 minutes

1

SALAD

1½ cups (200 g) pearl barley
3 tablespoons finely chopped fresh parsley
2 tablespoons finely chopped fresh mint
4 scallions (spring onions), finely chopped
2 tomatoes, chopped
1 red or green bell pepper (capsicum), finely diced

DRESSING

¼ cup (60 ml) extra-virgin olive oil
2 tablespoons freshly squeezed lemon juice
½ teaspoon salt
Freshly ground black pepper

1. **To prepare the salad,** cook the barley in salted boiling water until tender, 25–30 minutes.

2. **Drain** in a colander and rinse under cold running water. Drain again and dry in a clean kitchen towel.

3. **Transfer** the barley to a medium salad bowl and add the parsley, mint, scallions, tomatoes, and bell pepper.

4. **To prepare the dressing,** whisk the oil, lemon juice, salt, and pepper in a small bowl. Drizzle over the salad and toss well.

5. **Chill** for 30 minutes before serving.

AMOUNT PER SERVING	204	5g	1g	4g	46g	0.7g
NUTRITION FACTS	**CALORIES**	**PROTEIN**	**FAT**	**FIBER**	**CARBS**	**SALT**
PERCENT DAILY VALUES (based on 2 000 calories)	10%	11%	1%	16%	35%	12%

If you liked this recipe, you will love these as well.

spelt salad with tomatoes & feta

122

couscous with eggplant

124

bulgur salad

Enjoy this salad the traditional way by using crisp romaine (cos) lettuce leaves instead of forks to scoop up the fragrant mixture. You can also serve fresh pita bread on the side.

Serves 4

15 minutes

1 hour 30 minutes

 2

SALAD

- 1 cup (150 g) fine or medium bulgur
- 4 tablespoons finely chopped fresh parsley
- 3 tablespoons finely chopped fresh mint
- 4 scallions (spring onions), finely chopped
- 2 tomatoes, diced
- ½ green bell pepper (capsicum), finely chopped
- ½ red bell pepper (capsicum), finely chopped
  Romaine (cos) lettuce leaves, to serve

DRESSING

- ¼ cup (60 ml) extra-virgin olive oil
- 2 tablespoons freshly squeezed lemon juice
  Salt and freshly ground black pepper

1. **To prepare the salad,** put the bulgur in a medium bowl and add plenty of cold water to cover. Set aside for 1 hour.

2. **Drain** the bulgur in a colander lined with a clean kitchen towel. Scoop the bulgur up in the towel and squeeze out all the excess moisture.

3. **Transfer** the bulgur to a large salad bowl and toss with the parsley, mint, scallions, tomatoes, and bell peppers.

4. **To prepare the dressing,** whisk the oil, lemon juice, salt, and pepper in a small bowl. Drizzle over the salad. Toss well.

5. **Chill** in the refrigerator for 30 minutes before serving.

6. **Serve** with the cos lettuce leaves to scoop up the salad.

AMOUNT PER SERVING	279	5g	14g	8g	33g	0.2g
NUTRITION FACTS	CALORIES	PROTEIN	FAT	FIBER	CARBS	SALT
PERCENT DAILY VALUES (based on 2 000 calories)	13%	11%	17%	32%	25%	4%

If you liked this recipe, you will love these as well.

tabbouleh

 112

bulgur salad with zucchini flowers

 120

quinoa, corn & pinto bean salad

128

tuna barley salad

This is a healthy and filling dish that can be served for lunch or dinner.

Serves 6

30 minutes

30 minutes

45 minutes

3

SALAD

2 potatoes, unpeeled, cut in $\frac{1}{4}$-inch (5-mm) slices

1 tablespoon extra-virgin olive oil

Salt and freshly ground black pepper

2 teaspoons fresh rosemary

4 cups (1 liter) vegetable stock

1 teaspoon finely chopped fresh oregano

1 teaspoon finely chopped fresh marjoram

1 cup (200 g) pearl barley

1 red onion, sliced

8 ounces (250 g) green beans

6 tuna steaks, about 5 ounces (150 g) each

1 small bunch fresh parsley, finely chopped

8 ounces (250 g) roasted bell pepper (capsicum), sliced

2 firm ripe tomatoes, chopped

1 cup (100 g) black olives, finely chopped

DRESSING

$\frac{1}{2}$ cup (125 ml) vegetable stock

$\frac{1}{4}$ cup (60 ml) extra-virgin olive oil

4 cloves garlic, finely chopped

1 teaspoon mixed dried herbs

2 teaspoons Dijon mustard

1. **To prepare the salad,** preheat the oven to 425°F (220°C/gas 7). Brush the potatoes lightly with the oil and sprinkle with salt, pepper, and rosemary. Place on baking sheets and bake for 30 minutes or until tender, turning 2–3 times during cooking.

2. **Pour** the stock into a large saucepan and bring to a boil. Add the oregano, marjoram, and barley. Cover and simmer until the barley is tender, 25–30 minutes. Remove from the heat and set aside.

3. **Soak** the red onion in a small bowl of cold water for 30 minutes. Drain.

4. **Blanch** the green beans in boiling water for 2 minutes. Drain well.

5. **Season** the tuna steaks with salt and pepper and cook in a hot grill pan until tender, about 2 minutes each side. Chop the steaks into large chunks.

6. **To prepare the dressing,** whisk the stock, oil, garlic, herbs, and mustard in a small bowl.

7. **Mix** the green beans, onion, parsley, tomatoes, olives, and half the dressing with the warm barley. Season with salt and pepper and toss well.

8. **Set out** six serving dishes. Place several slices of potato in the center of each dish and top with a generous spoonful of barley mixture, roasted pepper, and tuna. Drizzle with the remaining dressing. Serve warm.

AMOUNT PER SERVING						
	520	41g	23g	4g	42g	1.7g
NUTRITION FACTS	CALORIES	PROTEIN	FAT	FIBER	CARBS	SALT
PERCENT DAILY VALUES (based on 2 000 calories)	25%	89%	28%	16%	32%	29%

bulgur salad
with zucchini flowers

Zucchini flowers have a wonderful flavor all their own. They are also very pretty and add an attractive finish to any dish. They are available in the summer at farmers' markets.

 Serves 6

 25 minutes

 1 hour

 1

2	cups (300 g) fine or medium bulgur
3	zucchini (courgettes), cut into thin batons
1	tablespoon freshly squeezed lemon juice
½	cup (125 g) pesto
¼	cup (50 g) pine nuts, toasted
⅓	cup (90 ml) extra-virgin

olive oil
Salt and freshly ground black pepper

2	bunches arugula (rocket)
½	teaspoon sweet paprika
6	very fresh zucchini (courgette) flowers, coarsely chopped

1. **To prepare the salad,** put the bulgur in a medium bowl and add plenty of cold water to cover. Set aside for 1 hour.

2. **Drain** the bulgur in a colander lined with a clean kitchen towel. Scoop the bulgur up in the towel and squeeze out all the excess moisture.

3. **Transfer** the bulgur into a salad bowl. Add the zucchini, lemon juice, pesto,

pine nuts, and 3 tablespoons of the oil. Season with salt and pepper and toss well.

4. **Arrange** the arugula in six individual serving dishes.

5. **Spoon** the salad on top of the arugula. Dust with the paprika and top with the zucchini flowers. Drizzle with the remaining oil and serve.

AMOUNT PER SERVING	474	12g	30g	9g	40g	0.2g
NUTRITION FACTS	**CALORIES**	**PROTEIN**	**FAT**	**FIBER**	**CARBS**	**SALT**
PERCENT DAILY VALUES (based on 2000 calories)	23%	26%	37%	36%	31%	4%

If you liked this recipe, you will love these as well.

spicy garbanzo bean salad with vegetables

94

new mexican chicken salad

246

spelt salad with tomatoes & feta

Spelt is an ancient strain of wheat that has suddenly become fashionable again. Buy the precooked variety; otherwise, you will need to soak it for several hours before cooking. Spelt is lower in gluten than many other types of wheat and can be easier to digest.

 Serves 4

15 minutes

5–10 minutes

40 minutes

1

1½	cups (200 g) spelt
24	cherry tomatoes, halved
2	cups (250 g) feta cheese, diced
6	scallions (spring onions), chopped
1	tablespoon finely chopped lemon zest
	Fresh basil leaves, torn

2	tablespoons capers, drained
	Salt and freshly ground black pepper
⅓	cup (90 ml) extra-virgin olive oil + extra, to serve
	Fresh mint leaves, chopped, to garnish
	Handful of black olives

1. **Cook** the spelt in salted boiling water until just tender. Follow the instructions on the package for the cooking time.

2. **Drain** and rinse under cold running water. Drain again and dry on a clean kitchen towel.

3. **Transfer** to a salad bowl. Add the tomatoes, feta, scallions, lemon zest, basil, capers, salt, pepper, and oil. Mix well and let rest for 5–10 minutes.

4. **Garnish** with mint and olives and serve with extra oil on the side.

AMOUNT PER SERVING	512	16g	34g	9g	37g	2.2g
NUTRITION FACTS	**CALORIES**	**PROTEIN**	**FAT**	**FIBER**	**CARBS**	**SALT**
PERCENT DAILY VALUES (based on 2 000 calories)	25%	35%	42%	36%	28%	36%

If you liked this recipe, you will love these as well.

raspberry, feta & walnut salad

46

chicken salad with parmesan & tomatoes

230

chicken, blue cheese & walnut salad

236

couscous with eggplant

When buying eggplant, always check that the skin is smooth and without any brown spots. The eggplant itself should feel heavy and firm and have a nice green stem end.

 Serves 4

 10 minutes

30 minutes

5–10 minutes

2

½ cup (125 ml) extra-virgin olive oil

2 medium eggplant (aubergines), with peel, diced
Salt and freshly ground black pepper

2 cups (300 g) instant couscous

2 cups (500 ml) boiling water

2 scallions (spring onions), finely sliced

2 tablespoons torn fresh basil + extra, to garnish

4 ripe tomatoes, chopped

2 tablespoons finely chopped fresh cilantro (coriander)

1 cup (125 g) freshly grated ricotta salata or Parmesan cheese

1. **Heat** 3 tablespoons of oil in a large frying pan over medium heat. Add the eggplant and sauté until tender, 5–10 minutes. Remove from the heat, season with salt and pepper, and let cool slightly.

2. **Put** the couscous in a large bowl. Pour in the water and 1 tablespoon of oil. Season with salt. Mix well and let rest for 10 minutes.

3. **Mix** the couscous with a fork to separate the grains. Add the scallions and basil.

4. **Put** the tomatoes in a small bowl. Season with salt and mix in 2 tablespoons of oil.

5. **Stir** the eggplant and tomatoes into the couscous.

6. **Spoon** the couscous salad into four individual serving bowls. Sprinkle with the cilantro and cheese and garnish with the extra basil. Drizzle with the remaining oil and serve.

AMOUNT PER SERVING	695	23g	40g	5g	61g	0.6g
NUTRITION FACTS	**CALORIES**	**PROTEIN**	**FAT**	**FIBER**	**CARBS**	**SALT**
PERCENT DAILY VALUES (based on 2 000 calories)	33%	50%	49%	20%	47%	10%

If you liked this recipe, you will love these as well.

marinated eggplant salad

64

couscous with oranges & pistachios

126

lamb & orange **couscous salad**

274

couscous with oranges & pistachios

Made from grain, couscous is a staple food in North Africa and many parts of the Middle East. According to Algerian folklore, it was invented by the Jinn (supernatural beings in Arabian mythology)!

Serves 6

20 minutes

10 minutes

1

SALAD

2	cups (500 ml) apple juice
2	cups (300 g) instant couscous
½	red bell pepper (capsicum), diced
4	tablespoons finely chopped fresh parsley
3	tablespoons finely chopped fresh mint
¼	cup (35 g) currants
2	oranges, peeled, halved, and broken into segments
1	small red onion, thinly sliced
⅓	cup (30 g) pistachios

DRESSING

	Freshly squeezed juice of 1 lemon or lime
	Freshly squeezed juice of 1 orange
2	tablespoons extra-virgin olive oil or walnut oil
2	teaspoons honey

1. **To prepare the salad,** pour the apple juice into a medium saucepan over medium heat and bring to a boil. Stir in the couscous. Remove from the heat. Cover and let cool.

2. **Fluff** the couscous up with a fork. Add the bell pepper, parsley, mint, and currants. Stir to combine.

3. **Transfer** to a salad bowl. Add the oranges, onion, and pistachios.

4. **To prepare the dressing,** combine the orange and lemon juice, oil, and honey in a small saucepan over low heat. Stir until the honey dissolves into the mixture—do not allow it to boil. Drizzle over the over the salad, toss gently, and serve.

AMOUNT PER SERVING	328	9g	8g	3g	56g	0.1g
NUTRITION FACTS	**CALORIES**	**PROTEIN**	**FAT**	**FIBER**	**CARBS**	**SALT**
PERCENT DAILY VALUES (based on 2 000 calories)	16%	20%	10%	12%	43%	2%

If you liked this recipe, you will love these as well.

spinach, grapefruit & pecorino **salad**

48

pink grapefruit & quinoa salad

130

warm steak salad with papaya & onion

272

quinoa, corn & pinto bean salad

Quinoa—pronounced *KEEN-wa*—is often called a superfood because it is high in protein, potassium, iron, magnesium, and lysine. It cooks in about 15 minutes.

 Serves 4

15 minutes

30 minutes

15 minutes

1

SALAD

1	cup (185 g) quinoa
2	cups (500 ml) water
2	red bell peppers (capsicums), diced
1	cup (180 g) canned pinto beans, drained and rinsed
1	cup (200 g) canned corn (sweet corn)
6	radishes, thinly sliced
1	scallion (spring onion), chopped

SPICY VINAIGRETTE

⅓	cup (90 ml) extra-virgin olive oil
2	tablespoons freshly squeezed lemon juice
2	tablespoons raspberry vinegar
1	tablespoon sherry
1	teaspoon finely grated lemon zest
½	teaspoon brown sugar
2	teaspoons horseradish cream
	Dash of Tabasco sauce

1. **Rinse** the quinoa thoroughly under cold running water. Drain well.

2. **Pour** the water into a medium saucepan and bring to a boil. Stir in the quinoa, reduce the heat, and cover. Simmer until the water is absorbed and the quinoa is cooked, about 15 minutes. Drain well and set aside to cool, about 30 minutes.

3. **To prepare the spicy vinaigrette,** whisk the oil, lemon juice, vinegar, sherry, lemon zest, brown sugar, horseradish cream, and Tabasco sauce in a small bowl.

4. **Combine** the quinoa, bell peppers, beans, corn, radishes, and scallion in a salad bowl. Drizzle with the dressing, toss gently, and serve.

AMOUNT PER SERVING	480	14g	25g	4g	53g	0.4g
NUTRITION FACTS	CALORIES	PROTEIN	FAT	FIBER	CARBS	SALT
PERCENT DAILY VALUES (based on 2 000 calories)	23%	30%	31%	16%	41%	6%

If you liked this recipe, you will love these as well.

pink grapefruit & quinoa salad

130

thai rice salad

160

pink grapefruit & quinoa salad

Quinoa has a natural coating of bitter-tasting saponin, which protects the seeds from birds and insects. While a lot of this is removed before you buy it, it pays to always rinse the quinoa thoroughly under cold running water. It should taste sweet, not bitter or soapy.

Serves 4

15 minutes

30 minutes

15 minutes

1

SALAD

1	cup (185 g) quinoa
2	cups (500 ml) apple juice
½	red bell pepper (capsicum), diced
4	tablespoons finely chopped fresh parsley
3	tablespoons finely chopped fresh mint
2	pink grapefruit, peeled, halved, and broken into segments
1	small onion, sliced

WARM CITRUS DRESSING

	Freshly squeezed juice of 1 grapefruit
2	tablespoons extra-virgin olive oil or hazelnut oil
1	teaspoon honey

1. **Rinse** the quinoa thoroughly under cold running water. Drain well.

2. **Bring** the apple juice to a boil in a medium saucepan over medium heat. Stir in the quinoa. Cover and simmer over low heat until the apple juice is absorbed and the quinoa is cooked, about 15 minutes. Drain well and set aside to cool, about 30 minutes.

3. **Transfer** the cooled quinoa to a salad bowl and add the bell pepper, parsley, mint, grapefruit, and onion. Toss well.

4. **To prepare the warm citrus dressing,** combine the grapefruit juice, oil, and honey in a small saucepan over low heat. Simmer until the honey is dissolved.

5. **Drizzle** the dressing over the salad, toss gently, and serve.

AMOUNT PER SERVING **NUTRITION FACTS** PERCENT DAILY VALUES (based on 2 000 calories)	307 CALORIES 15%	6g PROTEIN 13%	6g FAT 7%	10g FIBER 40%	58g CARBS 45%	0.2g SALT 4%

If you liked this recipe, you will love these as well.

orange & artichoke salad

36

shrimp & mango salad

206

sweet chile & pineapple salad

306

panzanella with tomato vinaigrette

This is a new take on a classic Tuscan salad made with bread and fresh summer vegetables.

Serves 4

30 minutes

25 minutes

20 minutes

2

SALAD

12	ounces (350 g) day-old, Italian-style bread, cut into cubes
2	tablespoons extra-virgin olive oil
1	tablespoon finely chopped fresh rosemary
1½	pounds (500 g) tomatoes
1	cucumber
12	large black olives, pitted
1	small red onion, finely chopped
12	basil leaves, torn
2	mint leaves, finely chopped
½	tablespoon finely chopped fresh marjoram

TOMATO VINAIGRETTE

2	medium tomatoes
⅓	cup (90 ml) extra-virgin olive oil
2	tablespoons red wine vinegar
1	tablespoon balsamic vinegar
2	cloves garlic
	Salt and freshly ground black pepper

1. **To prepare the salad**, preheat the oven to 400°F (200°C/gas 6). Toss the bread with the 2 tablespoons of oil and rosemary. Spread out on a baking sheet. Bake for 5 minutes until golden. Set aside to cool, about 15 minutes.

2. **Remove** the seeds from the tomatoes and chop into small chunks. Peel the cucumber and remove the seeds by running a teaspoon along the central seed area. Slice thinly.

3. **To prepare the dressing,** heat a small frying pan over medium heat.

Brush the skins of the tomatoes with a little oil. Sauté in the pan until very tender and well cooked.

4. **Chop** the sautéed tomatoes in a food processor with the remaining oil, both types of vinegar, garlic, salt, and pepper. Set aside.

5. **Combine** the bread cubes, tomatoes, cucumber, onion, olives, basil, mint, and marjoram in a large salad bowl. Drizzle with the tomato vinaigrette and toss well. Let sit for 10 minutes before serving.

AMOUNT PER SERVING	703 CALORIES	10g PROTEIN	51g FAT	4g FIBER	54g CARBS	1.7g SALT
NUTRITION FACTS						
PERCENT DAILY VALUES (based on 2000 calories)	34%	22%	63%	16%	42%	28%

rice noodle salad

This spicy little salad makes a perfect starter. Vary the amount of chiles according to taste.

 Serves 4

20 minutes

30 minutes

10 minutes

2

8	ounces (250 g) long, flat rice noodles
1	tablespoon sesame oil
1	(1-inch/2.5-cm) piece ginger, finely grated
2	small fresh red chiles, seeded and thinly sliced
1	red bell pepper (capsicum), cut in small pieces
6	scallions (spring onions), sliced on the diagonal
1	bunch fresh cilantro (coriander)
1/3	cup (90 ml) vegetable stock Freshly squeezed juice of 2 limes
2	tablespoons Japanese rice vinegar
2	tablespoons light soy sauce
1	teaspoon finely chopped lemon zest
3	tablespoons sesame seeds

1. **Cook** the rice noodles following the instructions on the package. Drain well and transfer to a salad bowl.

2. **Heat** the oil in a wok or frying pan over medium heat. Add the ginger and chiles and sauté for 2 minutes.

3. **Add** the bell pepper, raise the heat to medium-high, and stir-fry until softened, 2–3 minutes. Add the scallions and sauté for 2 minutes.

4. **Put** the bell pepper mixture in the salad bowl with the noodles. Add the cilantro and toss well.

5. **Whisk** the vegetable stock, lime juice, rice vinegar, soy sauce, and lemon zest in a small bowl. Drizzle over the noodles. Sprinkle with the sesame seeds and chill for 30 minutes before serving.

AMOUNT PER SERVING	327	6g	8g	1g	54g	1.2g
NUTRITION FACTS	**CALORIES**	**PROTEIN**	**FAT**	**FIBER**	**CARBS**	**SALT**
PERCENT DAILY VALUES (based on 2000 calories)	16%	12%	10%	4%	42%	20%

If you liked this recipe, you will love these as well.

thai noodle salad

136

thai beef salad

270

thai noodle salad

This salad has all the flavors of Asia. Make sure you use very fresh bean sprouts as they lose their delicate flavor very quickly.

Serves 4

15 minutes

1 hour 30 minutes

5 minutes

2

SALAD
12	ounces (350 g) dried vermicelli rice noodles
1	small cucumber, very thinly sliced
8	scallions (spring onions), finely chopped
2	carrots, cut into matchsticks
2	cups (100 g) bean sprouts
3	tablespoons finely chopped fresh cilantro (coriander)

DRESSING
5	tablespoons freshly squeezed lime juice
2	tablespoons Thai fish sauce
1	tablespoon light soy sauce
1	shallot, finely sliced
2	cloves garlic, finely chopped
1	small red chile, seeded and finely chopped
2	tablespoons palm sugar or light brown sugar

1. **To prepare the salad,** cook the rice noodles following the instructions on the package. Drain well and transfer to a salad bowl. Chill in the refrigerator for 30 minutes.

2. **Add** the cucumber, scallions, carrots, bean sprouts, and cilantro to the noodles in the bowl and toss gently.

3. **To prepare the dressing,** mix the lime juice, fish sauce, soy sauce, shallot, garlic, chile, and sugar in a small bowl until the sugar is dissolved.

4. **Drizzle** the dressing over the salad and toss well. Cover and refrigerate for at least 1 hour. Serve chilled.

AMOUNT PER SERVING	355	6g	0g	1g	80g	0.6g
NUTRITION FACTS	**CALORIES**	**PROTEIN**	**FAT**	**FIBER**	**CARBS**	**SALT**
PERCENT DAILY VALUES (based on 2 000 calories)	17%	13%	0%	4%	62%	9%

If you liked this recipe, you will love these as well.

crunchy lentil salad

96

thai calamari salad

216

thai fish & mango salad

218

greek orzo salad
with olives & pepper

Orzo, also known as risoni, are a tiny, rice-shaped type of pasta. In Italy risoni are mainly used in soups, but they also make an excellent base for salads.

 Serves 4

 30 minutes

 30 minutes

 1

SALAD
12	ounces (350 g) orzo
1	tablespoon extra-virgin olive oil
5	ounces (150 g) feta cheese, crumbled
1	red bell pepper (capsicum), finely chopped
1	yellow bell pepper (capsicum), finely chopped
1	green bell pepper (capsicum), finely chopped
1½	cups (150 g) Kalamata olives, pitted and chopped
4	scallions (spring onions), sliced
2	tablespoons capers, drained
3	tablespoons pine nuts, toasted

DRESSING
⅓	cup (90 ml) extra-virgin olive oil
	Freshly squeezed juice and zest of 2 lemons
1	tablespoon white wine vinegar
4	cloves garlic, finely chopped
1½	teaspoons dried oregano
1	teaspoon Dijon mustard
1	teaspoon ground cumin
	Salt and freshly ground black pepper

1. **To prepare the salad,** cook the orzo in a large saucepan of boiling salted water until al dente. Drain and rinse under cold running water. Drain again and dry on a kitchen towel.

2. **Transfer to** a salad bowl. Add the oil. Add the feta, bell peppers, olives, scallions, and capers and toss well.

3. **To prepare the dressing,** whisk the oil, lemon juice and zest, vinegar, garlic, oregano, mustard, cumin, salt, and pepper in a small bowl.

4. **Drizzle** the dressing over the salad and toss well. Top with the pine nuts and serve.

AMOUNT PER SERVING	755	20g	44g	6g	75g	3.4g
NUTRITION FACTS	**CALORIES**	**PROTEIN**	**FAT**	**FIBER**	**CARBS**	**SALT**
PERCENT DAILY VALUES (based on 2 000 calories)	36%	43%	54%	24%	58%	56%

If you liked this recipe, you will love these as well.

middle eastern bean & artichoke salad

100

pasta salad with tomatoes, basil & cheese

146

classic rice salad

168

fusilli & curry salad

The secret to perfect pasta lies in the cooking: bring a large saucepan of salted water to a boil; don't add the pasta until it is boiling vigorously and return to a boil as soon as possible. Cook until just tender, which is known as *al dente* (with just a little firmness left in the center).

Serves 4

15 minutes

1 hour

10 minutes

1

SALAD

1	pound (500 g) fusilli or rotini
1	red bell pepper (capsicum), chopped
1	green bell pepper (capsicum), chopped
4	ounces (120 g) lean ham, cut into thin strips
2	tablespoons snipped fresh chives

DRESSING

1/3	cup (90 ml) extra-virgin olive oil
2	tablespoons white wine vinegar
1/2	teaspoon sugar
1	teaspoon curry powder
	Salt and freshly ground black pepper

1. **To prepare the salad,** cook the pasta in a large saucepan of salted boiling water until al dente. Drain and rinse under cold running water. Drain again and dry on a clean kitchen towel.

2. **Put** the pasta in a salad bowl with the bell peppers, ham, and chives. Toss well.

3. **To prepare the dressing,** whisk the oil, vinegar, sugar, and curry in a small bowl. Season with salt and pepper.

4. **Drizzle** the dressing over the salad and toss well. Chill in the refrigerator for at least 1 hour before serving.

AMOUNT PER SERVING **NUTRITION FACTS** PERCENT DAILY VALUES (based on 2 000 calories)	671 **CALORIES** 32%	22g **PROTEIN** 48%	24g **FAT** 30%	5g **FIBER** 20%	98g **CARBS** 75%	0.9g **SALT** 15%

If you liked this recipe, you will love these as well.

spicy garbanzo bean salad with vegetables

94

pickled daikon noodle salad with shrimp

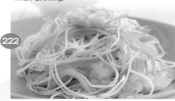
222

thai beef salad

270

pasta & bean salad

Use any ready-to-serve chili paste, such as sambal oelek or Thai chili paste.

- Serves 4
- 15 minutes
- 20 minutes

1

1	pound (500 g) orecchiette
1/4	cup (60 g) butter
2 1/4	cups (400 g) fresh or frozen fava (broad) beans
1	teaspoon crushed black peppercorns
1	teaspoon chili paste
2	cups (500 ml) chicken or vegetable stock
12	radishes, thinly sliced
4	tablespoons finely chopped fresh parsley
2	ounces (60 g) freshly grated Parmesan cheese

1. **Cook** the pasta in a large saucepan of salted boiling water until al dente. Drain and rinse under cold running water. Drain again and dry on a clean kitchen towel.

2. **Heat** the butter in a large frying pan over medium heat. Add the fava beans, peppercorns, and chili paste. Sauté for 3–4 minutes.

3. **Add** the stock and simmer until the fava beans are tender, about 5 minutes. Drain well.

4. **Combine** the pasta and fava bean mixture in a salad bowl. Add the radishes, parsley, and cheese. Toss well and serve warm.

AMOUNT PER SERVING	665 CALORIES	27g PROTEIN	20g FAT	10g FIBER	100g CARBS	0.6g SALT
NUTRITION FACTS PERCENT DAILY VALUES (based on 2 000 calories)	32%	59%	25%	40%	77%	10%

If you liked this recipe, you will love these as well.

pasta salad with tomatoes & croûtons

152

grilled bell pepper pasta salad

155

pasta salad with roasted garlic

Twenty cloves may sound like a lot of garlic, but after roasting, garlic takes on a wonderfully sweet and mild flavor.

Serves 6

15 minutes

30 minutes

2

20	cloves garlic, unpeeled	
8	slices bacon, rinds removed, chopped	
2	tablespoons butter	
2	cups (120 g) bread crumbs made from day-old bread	

4	tablespoons finely chopped fresh mixed herbs
	Freshly ground black pepper
1	pound (500 g) linguine

1. **Preheat** the oven to 400°F (200°C/gas 6). Place the garlic on a lightly oiled baking sheet. Bake until soft and golden, about 15 minutes. Peel the garlic and set aside.

2. **Sauté** the bacon in a large nonstick frying pan over a medium heat until crisp and golden, about 5 minutes. Drain on paper towels.

3. **Melt** the butter in a clean frying pan, add the bread crumbs, herbs, and

black pepper and sauté until the bread crumbs are golden, about 5 minutes.

4. **Meanwhile,** cook the pasta in a large saucepan of salted boiling water until al dente. Drain and rinse under cold running water. Drain again and dry on a clean kitchen towel.

5. **Put** the pasta in a salad bowl. Add the garlic, bacon, and bread crumb mixture, toss well, and serve.

AMOUNT PER SERVING **NUTRITION FACTS** PERCENT DAILY VALUES (based on 2,000 calories)	490 CALORIES 24%	20g PROTEIN 43%	12g FAT 15%	4g FIBER 16%	80g CARBS 62%	1.9g SALT 32%

If you liked this recipe, you will love these as well.

pasta & bean salad

142

pasta salad with tomatoes & basil

150

chicken waldorf salad with ranch dressing

250

pasta salad with tomatoes, basil & cheese

The crisp golden Parmesan adds a wonderful flavor to this salad. To toast the pine nuts, place them in a small pan over medium heat and cook until golden; shake the pan often during cooking so that they don't burn.

Serves 6

10 minutes

20 minutes

1

1	pound (500 g) cherry tomatoes, quartered
4	cloves garlic, finely chopped
1	small bunch basil, torn + extra, to garnish
⅓	cup (90 ml) extra-virgin olive oil
	Salt and freshly ground black pepper
1	cup (120 g) freshly grated Parmesan cheese
1	pound (500 g) penne
4	tablespoons pine nuts, toasted

1. **Combine** the tomatoes, garlic, basil, and oil in a salad bowl and mix well. Season with salt and pepper.

2. **Preheat** the oven to 425°F (220°C/gas 7). Line a baking sheet with parchment paper. Sprinkle the cheese onto the paper in a thin layer and bake until melted together and golden, about 5 minutes. Remove from the oven and let cool and crispen.

3. **Meanwhile,** cook the pasta in a large saucepan of salted boiling water until al dente. Drain and rinse under cold running water. Drain again and dry on a clean kitchen towel.

4. **Add** the pasta to the bowl with the tomato mixture. Toss well.

5. **Break** the baked cheese into pieces and arrange on the pasta. Garnish with the basil and pine nuts and serve.

AMOUNT PER SERVING	567	19g	27g	4g	65g	0.4g
NUTRITION FACTS	CALORIES	PROTEIN	FAT	FIBER	CARBS	SALT
PERCENT DAILY VALUES (based on 2000 calories)	27%	41%	33%	16%	50%	6%

If you liked this recipe, you will love these as well.

pasta salad with cheese & arugula
148

pasta salad with tomatoes & croûtons
152

bacon & egg salad with frisée
260

pasta salad with cheese & arugula

Substitute the same quantity of fresh mozzarella for the Emmental and add some finely chopped garlic for a slightly different but equally delicious salad.

 Serves 4

 15 minutes

 20 minutes

 1

1	pound (500 g) cherry tomatoes, chopped
1/3	cup (90 ml) extra-virgin olive oil
2	sprigs basil, torn
1/2	fresh red chile, seeded and finely chopped
	Salt

1	pound (500 g) rotini, or other short pasta
5	ounces (150 g) Emmental or Swiss cheese, very thinly sliced
1	cup (50 g) baby arugula (rocket) leaves

1. **Combine** the tomatoes, oil, basil, and chile in a salad bowl. Season with salt.

2. **Cook** the pasta in a large saucepan of salted boiling water until al dente. Drain and rinse under cold running water. Drain again and dry on a clean kitchen towel.

3. **Add** the pasta to the bowl with the tomato mixture. Toss well.

4. **Top** with the Emmental and arugula, toss gently, and serve.

AMOUNT PER SERVING	778	27g	34g	5g	97g	0.4g
NUTRITION FACTS	CALORIES	PROTEIN	FAT	FIBER	CARBS	SALT
PERCENT DAILY VALUES (based on 2 000 calories)	37%	59%	42%	20%	75%	7%

If you liked this recipe, you will love these as well.

arugula, corn & kiwi fruit salad

42

pasta salad with pickled vegetables & arugula

156

pasta salad with tomatoes & basil

To ripen tomatoes, place them in a brown paper bag and put in a dark spot. Do not put tomatoes in the sun to ripen since this softens them.

Serves 4

10 minutes

20 minutes

2	pounds (1 kg) ripe tomatoes, peeled and diced
2	cloves garlic, thinly sliced
10	leaves basil, torn
1/3	cup (90 ml) extra-virgin olive oil

1/2	teaspoon dried oregano
	Salt and freshly ground black pepper
1	pound (500 g) whole-wheat (wholemeal) fusilli or rotini

1. **Combine** the tomatoes, garlic, basil, oil, and oregano in a large bowl. Season with salt and pepper.

2. **Cook** the pasta in a large saucepan of salted boiling until al dente. Drain and rinse under cold running water. Drain well and dry on a clean kitchen towel.

3. **Add** the pasta to the bowl with the tomato mixture. Toss well.

AMOUNT PER SERVING NUTRITION FACTS PERCENT DAILY VALUES (based on 2 000 calories)	652 CALORIES 31%	17g PROTEIN 37%	23g FAT 28%	6g FIBER 24%	100g CARBS 77%	0.2g SALT 4%

If you liked this recipe, you will love these as well.

italian salad

56

mediterranean seafood salad

200

tuna pasta salad

224

pasta salad with tomatoes & croûtons

If pressed for time, buy ready-made croûtons and sprinkle over the finished salad.

 Serves 4

20 minutes

20 minutes

2

16 ounces (400 g) cherry tomatoes, halved
2 cloves garlic, thinly sliced
1 tablespoon finely chopped fresh marjoram
1 tablespoon caper berries, rinsed and drained
4 anchovy fillets, finely chopped
½ teaspoon dried oregano

Salt and freshly ground black pepper
5 tablespoons extra-virgin olive oil
12 ounces (350 g) trofie or other short, small pasta
⅓ cup (90 ml) sunflower oil
2 slices sesame seed or ordinary bread, cut into cubes

1. **Combine** the tomatoes, garlic, marjoram, caper berries, anchovies, and oregano in a large salad bowl. Season with salt and pepper. Add the oil and mix well.

2. **Cook** the pasta in a large saucepan of salted boiling until al dente. Drain and rinse under cold running water. Drain well and dry on a clean kitchen towel.

3. **Add** the pasta to the salad bowl with the tomato mixture and toss gently.

4. **Heat** the sunflower oil in a small frying pan over medium heat. Fry the bread until crisp and golden brown, 2–3 minutes. Drain on paper towels.

5. **Add** the croûtons to the salad. Toss gently and serve.

AMOUNT PER SERVING	677	14g	37g	5g	77g	0.6g
NUTRITION FACTS	CALORIES	PROTEIN	FAT	FIBER	CARBS	SALT
PERCENT DAILY VALUES (based on 2000 calories)	33%	30%	46%	20%	59%	10%

If you liked this recipe, you will love these as well.

pasta salad with tomatoes & basil

150

bread salad with poached trout

196

grilled bell pepper pasta salad

Broiling the bell peppers intensifies their flavor. You can also grill the bell peppers on a barbecue or roast in the oven until blackened.

 Serves 6

30 minutes

40–45 minutes

30 minutes

2

3	large red bell peppers (capsicum)
3	large yellow bell peppers (capsicum)
¼	cup (60 ml) extra-virgin olive oil
	Salt and freshly ground black pepper

2	tablespoons capers, rinsed
2	anchovy fillets, chopped
1	tablespoon raisins, soaked in warm water for 5 minutes
1	tablespoon pine nuts
1	pound (500 g) rigatoni or other short pasta

1. **Place** the bell peppers under a hot broiler (grill) and broil until the skins are blistered and black all over.

2. **Transfer** to a plastic bag, close tightly and leave for 10–15 minutes (this loosens the skins further and makes peeling easier).

3. **Remove** the skin with your fingers when cool enough to handle. Cut the peppers in half and remove the stems and seeds. Cut the soft flesh into bite-sized pieces and arrange in a large shallow dish.

4. **Mix** the oil, salt, pepper, capers, anchovies, raisins, and pine nuts in a small bowl. Spread this mixture over the peppers. Let rest for 30 minutes.

5. **Cook** the pasta in a large saucepan of salted boiling water until al dente. Drain and rinse under cold running water. Drain again and dry on a clean kitchen towel.

6. **Transfer** the pasta to a salad bowl. Add the bell pepper mixture and serve.

AMOUNT PER SERVING NUTRITION FACTS PERCENT DAILY VALUES (based on 2 000 calories)	450 CALORIES 22%	13g PROTEIN 28%	13g FAT 16%	5g FIBER 20%	74g CARBS 57%	0.1g SALT 2%

If you liked this recipe, you will love these as well.

italian salad

56

jumbo shrimp salad

198

pasta salad with pickled vegetables and arugula

Ready-to-eat pickled vegetables are normally sold in glass jars and are made up of a mixture of cauliflower, shallots, peppers, garlic, and beans in a cider vinegar brine.

 Serves 6

 30 minutes

 30 minutes

 15 minutes

 1

1	pound (500 g) whole-wheat (wholemeal) pasta shells
1/8	teaspoon saffron strands
1/4	cup (60 ml) extra-virgin olive oil
1	bunch arugula (rocket)
1	tablespoon finely chopped fresh marjoram
1	tablespoon capers, drained
1	(8-ounce/250-g) jar pickled vegetables, drained and chopped
1/4	cup (60 g) mushrooms, in oil, drained and sliced

1. **Cook** the pasta in a large saucepan of salted boiling water for 5 minutes.

2. **Add** the saffron and cook until the pasta is al dente, 5–7 minutes more. Drain well. Transfer to a large salad bowl and drizzle with 1 tablespoon of oil. Let cool completely, about 30 minutes.

3. **Add** the arugula, marjoram, capers, pickled vegetables, and mushrooms to the bowl with the pasta. Drizzle with the remaining oil. Toss well and serve.

AMOUNT PER SERVING	365	12g	11g	8g	58g	0.7g
NUTRITION FACTS	CALORIES	PROTEIN	FAT	FIBER	CARBS	SALT
PERCENT DAILY VALUES (based on 2000 calories)	18%	26%	14%	32%	45%	12%

If you liked this recipe, you will love these as well.

arugula & pineapple salad

58

butternut squash with scallions

182

pasta salad with snow peas & salami

Make this crisp salad in the summer months when snow peas are at their best. Dress with a light vinaigrette that will enhance the snow peas' flavor.

Serves 4

10 minutes

15 minutes

15 minutes

1

SALAD

8   ounces (250 g) small pasta shells

6   ounces (180 g) snow peas (mangetout), trimmed

4   ounces (120 g) Italian salami, sliced

1   carrot, cut into matchsticks

4   ounces (120 g) mozzarella cheese, shredded

DRESSING

⅓   cup (90 ml) extra-virgin olive oil

2   tablespoons freshly squeezed lemon juice

     Salt and freshly ground black pepper

1. **To prepare the salad,** cook the pasta in a large saucepan of salted boiling water until al dente. Drain and rinse under cold running water. Drain again and dry on a clean kitchen towel.

2. **Plunge** the snow peas into a saucepan of lightly salted boiling water. When the water returns to a boil, simmer for 30 seconds, then drain. Refresh under cold running water. Drain again and dry on a kitchen towel.

3. **Combine** the pasta, snow peas, salami, carrot, and mozzarella in a large serving bowl.

4. **To prepare the dressing,** whisk the oil, lemon juice, salt, and pepper in a small bowl.

5. **Drizzle** the dressing over the salad and toss well. Chill for 15 minutes before serving.

AMOUNT PER SERVING	624	21g	39g	3g	50g	1.6g
NUTRITION FACTS	**CALORIES**	**PROTEIN**	**FAT**	**FIBER**	**CARBS**	**SALT**
PERCENT DAILY VALUES (based on 2 000 calories)	30%	46%	48%	12%	38%	26%

If you liked this recipe, you will love these as well.

melon, zucchini & pancetta **salad**

28

fennel sausage with zucchini

264

thai rice salad

Most of the ingredients in this salad are readily available at Asian food stores or markets. If you can't find the kaffir lime leaves, just leave them out.

 Serves 6

20 minutes

1 hour

10 minutes

1

SALAD

2	cups (400 g) Thai rice
5	scallions (spring onions) thinly sliced on the diagonal
3	carrots, finely grated
4	baby bok choy, chopped
2	kaffir lime leaves
½	cup coarsely chopped fresh cilantro (coriander)
1½	cups (250 g) coarsely chopped roasted peanuts
1	tablespoon black sesame seeds
2	tablespoons finely chopped fresh Thai or Italian basil

DRESSING

2	tablespoons peanut oil
	Freshly squeezed juice of 2 limes
3	tablespoons Thai fish sauce
2	tablespoons palm sugar or light brown sugar
2	tablespoons Thai sweet chili sauce
1	tablespoon finely grated ginger
	Pinch of chile powder or cayenne pepper
	Salt and freshly ground black pepper

1. **To prepare the salad**, bring a medium pot of salted water to a boil. Add the rice and simmer until tender, about 10 minutes. Drain and rinse under cold running water. Drain again and dry on a clean kitchen towel.

2. **Put** the rice in a large bowl. Add the scallions, carrots, bok choy, kaffir lime leaves, cilantro, peanuts, sesame seeds, and basil and toss well.

3. **To prepare the dressing**, whisk the oil, lime juice, fish sauce, sugar, chili sauce, ginger, chile powder, salt, and pepper in a small bowl.

4. **Drizzle** over the rice mixture and toss well. Chill in the refrigerator for 1 hour. Remove the kaffir lime leaves just before serving.

AMOUNT PER SERVING	578	17g	27g	4g	71g	0.5g
NUTRITION FACTS	CALORIES	PROTEIN	FAT	FIBER	CARBS	SALT
PERCENT DAILY VALUES (based on 2 000 calories)	28%	37%	33%	16%	55%	9%

If you liked this recipe, you will love these as well.

classic rice salad

168

pickled daikon noodle salad with shrimp

222

thai beef salad

270

mixed rice salad

If short of time, use a quick-cooking brown rice. Feel free to add other types of dried fruit and nuts to this nutritious salad.

 Serves 4

20 minutes

30 minutes

40 minutes

2

SALAD

½	cup (100 g) wild rice
½	cup (100 g) brown rice
½	cup (100 g) basmati rice
4	tablespoons snipped fresh chives
2	tablespoons finely chopped fresh parsley
6	dried apricots, coarsely chopped
1	cup (120 g) walnuts, coarsely chopped

DRESSING

3	tablespoons walnut oil
3	tablespoons extra-virgin olive oil
2	tablespoons white wine vinegar
1	tablespoon freshly squeezed lemon juice
½	teaspoon light brown sugar
1	teaspoon Dijon mustard
	Salt and freshly ground black pepper

1. **To prepare the salad,** cook the three types of rice in separate pans of salted boiling water until just tender. Follow the cooking times suggested on each package.

2. **Drain** each type of rice and let cool, about 30 minutes.

3. **Combine** the three types of rice in a salad bowl. Add the chives, parsley, apricots, and walnuts and mix well.

4. **To prepare the dressing,** whisk both types of oil, the vinegar, lemon juice, sugar, and mustard in a small bowl. Season with salt and pepper.

5. **Drizzle** the dressing over the salad. Toss well and serve.

AMOUNT PER SERVING	665	11g	41g	9g	65g	0.2g
NUTRITION FACTS	CALORIES	PROTEIN	FAT	FIBER	CARBS	SALT
PERCENT DAILY VALUES (based on 2000 calories)	32%	24%	51%	36%	50%	4%

If you liked this recipe, you will love these as well.

thai rice salad

160

woodland salad with raspberries & wild rice

166

rice salad with apple & walnuts

Frisée has an assertive flavor that blends with the rice base in this salad and works beautifully with the Gorgonzola, apples, and walnuts.

 Serves 6

15 minutes

15 minutes

1

1½ cups (300 g) long-grain rice
1 head frisée (curly endive), coarsely chopped
5 ounces (150 g) Gorgonzola cheese, cut into cubes
2 stalks celery, thinly sliced
2 Granny Smith apples, cored and cut into cubes
⅓ cup (90 ml) extra-virgin olive oil

Freshly squeezed juice of 1 lemon
1 fresh red chile, seeded and finely chopped
¼ cup (45 g) raisins
¼ teaspoon cumin seeds
16 walnuts, coarsely chopped

1. **Cook** the rice in a large pot of salted boiling water until tender, about 15 minutes.

2. **Drain** and cool under cold running water. Drain again and dry in a clean kitchen towel.

3. **Put** the rice in a large salad bowl and add the frisée, Gorgonzola, celery, apples, oil, lemon juice, chile, raisins, cumin, and walnuts. Toss gently and serve.

AMOUNT PER SERVING	567	13g	36g	2g	51g	0.5g
NUTRITION FACTS	CALORIES	PROTEIN	FAT	FIBER	CARBS	SALT
PERCENT DAILY VALUES (based on 2 000 calories)	27%	28%	44%	8%	39%	8%

If you liked this recipe, you will love these as well.

blue cheese & pecan salad

22

apple salad with yogurt dressing

24

apple, nut & celery salad

40

woodland salad with raspberries & wild rice

Serve this salad in the summer and fall when locally grown salad greens and raspberries are at their best.

Serves 6

20 minutes

30 minutes

40 minutes

1

SALAD
½	cup (100 g) brown rice
1	cup (200 g) wild rice
4	cups (200 g) mixed salad greens
1	bunch arugula (rocket), chopped
1	bunch watercress, chopped
1	tablespoon finely chopped fresh mint
1	tablespoon finely chopped fresh parsley
2	carrots, finely grated

VINAIGRETTE
2	cups (300 g) fresh raspberries
½	cup (125 ml) extra-virgin olive oil
2	tablespoons freshly squeezed lemon juice
	Salt and freshly ground black pepper

1. **To prepare the salad,** cook both types of rice in separate pans of salted boiling water until just tender. Follow the cooking times suggested on each package.

2. **Drain** each type of rice and let cool, about 30 minutes.

3. **Combine** both types of rice in a large bowl. Add all the salad greens, the watercress, mint, parsley, and carrots and toss well.

4. **To prepare the vinaigrette,** crush about 15 raspberries in a small bowl. Add the oil and lemon juice and season with salt and pepper. Whisk well.

5. **Garnish** the salad with the remaining raspberries.

6. **Drizzle** the vinaigrette over the salad and toss lightly. Divide the salad among six individual bowls and serve.

AMOUNT PER SERVING	380	5g	21g	4g	46g	0.2g
NUTRITION FACTS	CALORIES	PROTEIN	FAT	FIBER	CARBS	SALT
PERCENT DAILY VALUES (based on 2 000 calories)	18%	11%	26%	16%	35%	4%

If you liked this recipe, you will love these as well.

arugula & pineapple salad

58

mixed rice salad

162

classic rice salad

Vary the ingredients in this salad according to what you have in the garden or in your refrigerator. Replace the white rice with brown rice, if preferred.

 Serves 4

30 minutes

10 minutes

15 minutes

1

- 2 cups (400 g) short-grain rice
- 1 cup (150 g) frozen peas
- 20 cherry tomatoes, halved
- 4 ounces (125 g) Fontina or Emmental cheese, cut into small cubes
- 1 cucumber, peeled and cut into small cubes
- 2 tablespoons capers, drained
- 15 black olives, pitted and coarsely chopped
- 1 sweet red onion, chopped

 Fresh basil leaves, torn
- 1/4 cup (60 ml) extra-virgin olive oil

 Salt

1. **Cook** the rice in a large pot of salted boiling water until just tender, about 15 minutes.

2. **Drain** and cool under cold running water. Drain again and dry in a clean kitchen towel.

3. **Place** the peas in a small pot of salted boiling water and simmer until tender, about 5 minutes.

4. **Drain** and cool under cold running water. Drain again thoroughly.

5. **Combine** the rice, peas, tomatoes, cheese, cucumber, capers, olives, onion, and basil in a large salad bowl.

6. **Drizzle** with the oil and season with salt. Toss gently. Let rest for 10 minutes before serving.

AMOUNT PER SERVING NUTRITION FACTS PERCENT DAILY VALUES (based on 2000 calories)	686 CALORIES 33%	20g PROTEIN 43%	28g FAT 35%	5g FIBER 20%	94g CARBS 72%	1.7g SALT 28%

If you liked this recipe, you will love these as well.

rice salad with apple & walnuts

164

woodland salad with raspberries & wild rice

166

calabrian salad

This simple potato salad comes from Calabria, in southern Italy. Soaking the onions in cold water makes them milder; if you love the spicy flavor of fresh onions, just skip this step.

Serves 4

15 minutes

30 minutes

20 minutes

2

SALAD

3   red onions, peeled and sliced thinly

6   medium potatoes, unpeeled

8   firm plum tomatoes, sliced

15 fresh basil leaves, torn

1   tablespoon fresh oregano sprigs

DRESSING

½   cup (125 ml) extra-virgin olive oil

3   tablespoons white or red wine vinegar

Salt and freshly ground black pepper

1. **To prepare the salad,** put the onions in a bowl of cold water and let soak for 30 minutes. Drain well.

2. **Cook** the potatoes in salted boiling water until tender, about 20 minutes. Drain and set aside until just cool enough to handle. Slip off the skins and slice thinly.

3. **Arrange** slices of potatoes, tomatoes, and onions on four serving plates. Top with basil and oregano.

4. **To prepare the dressing,** whisk the oil, vinegar, salt, and pepper in a small bowl.

5. **Drizzle** some of the dressing over each portion and serve.

AMOUNT PER SERVING NUTRITION FACTS PERCENT DAILY VALUES (based on 2000 calories)	359 CALORIES 17%	3g PROTEIN 7%	29g FAT 36%	4g FIBER 16%	23g CARBS 18%	0.2g SALT 4%

If you liked this recipe, you will love these as well.

potato salad with bacon

176

chicken & potato salad

228

artichoke & potato salad
with lemon mayonnaise

Be sure to use the choicest new potatoes in this salad.

 Serves 4

15 minutes

30 minutes

15–20 minutes

2

2 fresh artichoke hearts, cut into thin wedges, or 12 ounces (350 g) marinated artichoke hearts, drained and quartered

1 pound (500 g) new potatoes, unpeeled

6 pitted black olives, sliced

2 scallions (spring onions), chopped

½ cup (125 ml) mayonnaise

2 tablespoons freshly squeezed lemon juice

Salt and freshly ground black pepper

1. **If using fresh** artichokes, cook in a saucepan of salted boiling water until tender, 10–15 minutes. Drain and let cool, about 30 minutes.

2. **Cook** the potatoes in a saucepan of salted boiling water until tender, 15–20 minutes. Drain, cool slightly, then cut into pieces of similar size to the artichokes. Set aside to cool.

3. **Combine** the artichokes, potatoes, olives, and scallions in a salad bowl.

4. **Mix** the mayonnaise and lemon juice in a small bowl. Pour over the salad and toss lightly to coat. Season with salt and pepper.

5. **Serve** at room temperature or lightly chilled.

AMOUNT PER SERVING	312	5g	25g	2g	20g	0.7g
NUTRITION FACTS	**CALORIES**	**PROTEIN**	**FAT**	**FIBER**	**CARBS**	**SALT**
PERCENT DAILY VALUES (based on 2 000 calories)	15%	11%	31%	8%	15%	12%

If you liked this recipe, you will love these as well.

blue cheese potato salad

174

grilled potato salad

178

blue cheese potato salad

The flavoring for this simple salad is prepared the day before and left overnight in the refrigerator for the aromas to meld and deepen.

Serves 6

30 minutes

13 hours

25 minutes

1

5	scallions (green onions), sliced
2	stalks celery, chopped
3	tablespoons finely chopped fresh parsley
½	cup (125 ml) mayonnaise
½	cup (125 ml) crème fraîche or sour cream
1	tablespoon freshly squeezed lemon juice

	Salt and freshly ground black pepper
5	ounces (150 g) blue cheese, crumbled
2	pounds (1 kg) red or yellow potatoes, unpeeled

1. **Combine** the scallions, celery, parsley, mayonnaise, crème fraîche, lemon juice, salt, and pepper in a bowl and mix well. Stir in the blue cheese. Cover the bowl and chill in the refrigerator overnight.

2. **Cook** the potatoes in a large pot of lightly salted boiling water until tender, about 25 minutes. Drain and set aside to cool.

3. **Dice** the potatoes into bite-sized pieces and transfer to a salad bowl. Pour the cheese mixture over the top, mix carefully, and serve.

AMOUNT PER SERVING NUTRITION FACTS PERCENT DAILY VALUES (based on 2000 calories)	391 CALORIES 19%	10g PROTEIN 22%	26g FAT 32%	3g FIBER 12%	30g CARBS 23%	0.7g SALT 12%

If you liked this recipe, you will love these as well.

pear roquefort & radicchio salad

32

mozzarella & tomato salad

60

chicken, blue cheese & walnut salad

236

potato salad with bacon

For best results, use good-quality bacon for this recipe.

 Serves 4

 30 minutes

 3 hours

 15 minutes

 2

SALAD

20   small new potatoes

6   slices bacon, rinds removed

2   tablespoons coarsely chopped fresh parsley

DRESSING

⅓   cup (90 ml) extra-virgin olive oil

3   tablespoons white wine vinegar

½   teaspoon Dijon mustard

Salt and freshly ground black pepper

4   scallions (spring onions), thinly sliced

1   small red onion, thinly sliced

1. **To prepare the salad,** cook the potatoes in salted boiling water until just tender, about 10 minutes. Drain well and cut in half.

2. **Sauté** the bacon in a frying pan over medium heat until crisp and golden, about 5 minutes. Drain on paper towels.

3. **To prepare the dressing,** whisk the oil, vinegar, mustard, salt, and pepper in a small bowl. Stir in the scallions and onion.

4. **Combine** the potatoes, bacon, and parsley in a salad bowl. Drizzle with the dressing and toss well to combine.

5. **Chill** in the refrigerator for 2 hours. Let sit at room temperature for about 1 hour before serving.

AMOUNT PER SERVING	432	11g	28g	4g	35g	1.8g
NUTRITION FACTS	**CALORIES**	**PROTEIN**	**FAT**	**FIBER**	**CARBS**	**SALT**
PERCENT DAILY VALUES (based on 2000 calories)	21%	24%	35%	16%	27%	30%

If you liked this recipe, you will love these as well.

artichoke & potato salad with lemon mayonnaise

172

potato & smoked sausage salad

262

grilled potato salad

This dish is great for barbecues because it can be prepared ahead of time and left to marinate in the refrigerator until just before cooking.

Serves 4

30 minutes

3–4 hours

20 minutes

2

6	large potatoes, peeled
¼	cup (60 ml) extra-virgin olive oil
2	cloves garlic, finely chopped
½	cup (50 g) pitted black olives
½	cup (125 ml) mayonnaise
⅔	cup (150 g) sour cream
2	tablespoons pesto

1. **Partially cook** the potatoes in salted boiling water for 10 minutes. Drain well.

2. **Cut** the potatoes into 1-inch (2.5-cm) cubes and put in a bowl. Combine the oil and garlic in a small bowl, then drizzle over the potatoes. Marinate in the refrigerator for 3–4 hours.

3. **Grill** the potatoes over a hot barbecue (on a vegetable grill rack set over the grill grate) or under a hot broiler (grill), turning until golden brown, crisp, and cooked through.

4. **Put** the potatoes in a salad bowl with the olives.

5. **Mix** the mayonnaise, sour cream, and pesto in a small bowl.

6. **Serve** the potatoes hot, with the mayonnaise mixture spooned over the top.

AMOUNT PER SERVING	628	8g	49g	4g	41g	1.2g
NUTRITION FACTS	**CALORIES**	**PROTEIN**	**FAT**	**FIBER**	**CARBS**	**SALT**
PERCENT DAILY VALUES (based on 2000 calories)	30%	17%	60%	16%	32%	19%

If you liked this recipe, you will love these as well.

chicken & potato salad

228

barbecued lamb salad

276

moroccan vegetable salad

Always check the freshness of your dried herbs and spices. While they may still be safe to eat after their best-by date, they do lose a great deal of flavor.

Serves 4

30 minutes

2–3 hours

1 hour

2

SPICY LIME MARINADE

1 teaspoon ground turmeric
1 teaspoon ground cumin
1 teaspoon ground cinnamon
½ teaspoon harissa or other chili paste
2 cloves garlic, finely chopped
½ cup (125 ml) extra-virgin olive oil
3 tablespoons freshly squeezed lime juice
1 tablespoon honey

SALAD

10 pearl onions, peeled
10 cloves garlic, peeled
3 carrots, cut into 2-inch (5-cm) lengths

1 bulb fennel, cut into wedges
4 parsnips, halved, then cut into quarters lengthwise
1 pound (500 g) sweet potatoes, cut into 1-inch (2.5-cm) pieces

HERBED YOGURT

1 cup (250 ml) plain yogurt
2 tablespoons finely chopped fresh dill
2 tablespoons finely chopped fresh mint
Salt and freshly ground black pepper

1. **To prepare the spicy lime marinade,** whisk the turmeric, cumin, cinnamon, harissa, garlic, oil, lime juice, and honey in a glass or ceramic bowl.

2. **To prepare the salad,** add the onions, garlic, carrots, fennel, parsnips, and sweet potatoes to the marinade and toss to coat. Cover and marinate in the refrigerator for 2–3 hours.

3. **To prepare the herbed yogurt,** whisk the yogurt, dill, and mint in a

small bowl. Season with salt and pepper. Cover and refrigerate until required.

4. **Preheat** the oven to 350°F (180°C/gas 4). Transfer the vegetables and their marinade to a baking dish. Bake until the vegetables are tender, about 1 hour.

6. **Serve** warm or at room temperature with the herbed yogurt.

AMOUNT PER SERVING	486 CALORIES 23%	8g PROTEIN 17%	30g FAT 37%	8g FIBER 32%	49g CARBS 38%	0.3g SALT 5%
NUTRITION FACTS						
PERCENT DAILY VALUES (based on 2 000 calories)						

butternut squash with scallions

Butternut squash (pumpkin), has a sweet, nutty flavor. The scallion dressing gives this salad a fresh tangy finish.

 Serves 6

 15 minutes

 35–45 minutes

 2

SALAD

2	pounds (1 kg) butternut squash (pumpkin), peeled and chopped
12	ounces (350 g) yellow or green baby summer squash
3	carrots, halved lengthwise
	Finely grated zest of 2 limes
1	tablespoon extra-virgin olive oil
	Freshly ground black pepper
5	ounces (150 g) feta cheese, crumbled

SCALLION DRESSING

12	scallions (spring onions), sliced
3	mild fresh green chiles, sliced
½	cup (125 ml) extra-virgin olive oil
¼	cup (90 ml) apple cider vinegar
2	tablespoons freshly squeezed lime juice
	Salt and freshly ground black pepper

1. **To prepare the salad,** preheat the oven to 350°F (180°C/gas 4).

2. **Place** both types of squash, the carrots, lime zest, oil, and black pepper in a baking dish. Toss to combine and bake until the vegetables are golden and soft, 35–45 minutes.

3. **To prepare the scallion dressing,** whisk the scallions, chiles, oil, vinegar, lime juice, salt, and pepper in a small bowl.

4. **Place** the vegetables in a serving dish. Season with pepper and top with the feta. Drizzle with the dressing and serve.

AMOUNT PER SERVING	342	7g	26g	4g	21g	0.9g
NUTRITION FACTS	**CALORIES**	**PROTEIN**	**FAT**	**FIBER**	**CARBS**	**SALT**
PERCENT DAILY VALUES (based on 2 000 calories)	16%	15%	32%	16%	16%	15%

If you liked this recipe, you will love these as well.

roasted beets with balsamic vinegar

roasted beets with orange & fennel

66

68

Deep
Blue Sea

grilled baby octopus salad

Be sure to cook the baby octopus on a very hot barbecue or grill pan for no more than 2–3 minutes. If you cook them longer, they will become rubbery.

Serves 4

20 minutes

4–12 hours

2–3 minutes

2

12 ounces (350 g) fresh baby octopus or calamari, cleaned
⅓ cup (90 ml) Thai sweet chili sauce
2 tablespoons freshly squeezed lime juice
1 tablespoon Thai fish sauce
1 tablespoon sesame oil
2 cups (100 g) mixed salad greens

1 cup (50 g) bean sprouts
1 cucumber, with peel, thinly sliced
8 ounces (250 g) cherry tomatoes, halved
½ cup chopped fresh cilantro (coriander)
Lime wedges, to serve

1. **Put** the baby octopus in a shallow glass or ceramic bowl.

2. **To prepare the marinade,** whisk the sweet chili sauce, lime juice, fish sauce, and sesame oil in a small bowl.

3. **Pour** the marinade over the octopus, cover with plastic wrap (cling film), and marinate for 4 hours or overnight. Drain and reserve the marinade.

4. **Divide** the salad greens evenly among four serving plates. Top with the bean sprouts, cucumber, and tomatoes.

5. **Preheat** a barbecue vegetable plate or grill pan to very hot. Add the baby octopus all at once and toss until cooked through, 2–3 minutes. Remove and set aside. Do not overcook.

6. **Place** the reserved marinade in a small saucepan and bring to a boil.

7. **Arrange** the baby octopus on top of the salad. Drizzle with the hot marinade and garnish with the cilantro and lime wedges. Serve at once.

AMOUNT PER SERVING						
NUTRITION FACTS	122	17g	4g	1g	4g	1.3g
PERCENT DAILY VALUES (based on 2 000 calories)	CALORIES	PROTEIN	FAT	FIBER	CARBS	SALT
	6%	37%	5%	4%	3%	21%

shrimp salad with avocados

You can improve the flavor of shrimp by brining them: dissolve 1 cup (250 g) of salt and ½ cup (100 g) of sugar in 2 cups (500 ml) of boiling water. Pour into a large bowl of iced water. Add the shrimp and let sit for 2 hours.

Serves 4

20 minutes

2 hours

3-5 minutes

2

SALAD
- 12 spears asparagus
- 2 cups (100 g) mixed salad greens
- 2 large tomatoes, chopped
- 1 bunch radishes, thinly sliced
- 2 avocados, peeled and cubed
- 2 tablespoons extra-virgin olive oil
- 30 scampi or jumbo shrimp (king prawns), shelled and deveined

DRESSING
- $\frac{1}{3}$ cup (90 ml) extra-virgin olive oil
- Freshly squeezed juice of 1 lemon
- Salt and freshly ground white pepper

1. **Cook** the asparagus in salted boiling water until just tender, 2–4 minutes, depending on the thickness.

2. **To prepare the salad,** arrange the salad greens, tomatoes, radishes, avocados, and asparagus on four individual serving plates.

3. **Heat** the oil in a large frying pan over medium-high heat. Sauté the shrimp until just cooked, 2–5 minutes depending on their size.

4. **To prepare the dressing,** whisk the oil and lemon juice in a small bowl. Season with salt and pepper.

5. **Arrange** the shrimp on top of the salads. Drizzle with the dressing and serve.

AMOUNT PER SERVING	434	14g	40g	4g	5g	0.2g
NUTRITION FACTS	CALORIES	PROTEIN	FAT	FIBER	CARBS	SALT
PERCENT DAILY VALUES (based on 2000 calories)	21%	30%	49%	16%	4%	4%

If you liked this recipe, you will love these as well.

jumbo shrimp salad

198

mixed seafood salad

202

crab salad with fennel

To prepare the fennel, slice off the leafy tops and roots and peel off the tough outer layer of leaves.

 Serves 4

20 minutes

2

DRESSING

2 large tomatoes

5 tablespoons extra-virgin olive oil

$\frac{1}{4}$ cup (60 ml) light (single) cream

1 tablespoon white wine vinegar

1 teaspoon finely chopped fresh tarragon

Pinch of superfine (caster) sugar

Dash of Worcestershire sauce

Salt and freshly ground black pepper

1 (2-inch/5-cm) piece cucumber, peeled and diced

SALAD

8 ounces (250 g) crabmeat

1 large bulb fennel, thinly sliced,

2 cups (100 g) mixed salad greens

1 tablespoon snipped fresh chives

Sweet paprika, to dust

1. **To prepare the dressing**, place the tomatoes in a medium bowl and cover with boiling water. Leave for 30 seconds, then remove the skins. Cut in half and squeeze out as many seeds as possible, and cut into small dice.

2. **Whisk** the oil, cream, vinegar, tarragon, sugar, Worcestershire sauce, salt, and pepper in a small bowl. Stir in the tomatoes and cucumber.

3. **To prepare the salad**, mix the crabmeat and fennel in a medium bowl and add half the creamy dressing.

4. **Arrange** the salad greens on four serving plates and top with the crab mixture. Spoon the remaining dressing over the top. Sprinkle with the chives, dust with the paprika, and serve.

AMOUNT PER SERVING	223	13g	18g	2g	3g	1.4g
NUTRITION FACTS	**CALORIES**	**PROTEIN**	**FAT**	**FIBER**	**CARBS**	**SALT**
PERCENT DAILY VALUES (based on 2000 calories)	11%	28%	22%	8%	2%	23%

If you liked this recipe, you will love these as well.

warm fennel & asparagus **salad**

34

pickled daikon noodle salad with **shrimp**

222

mixed beans with tuna

Four-bean mix is normally a combination of red kidney beans, garbanzo beans (chickpeas), soy beans, and butter beans—a perfect base for healthy salads. It doesn't really matter though; use a can of just one type of bean, or two small different-colored ones.

 Serves 4

 10 minutes

 1

1	cup (200 g) canned red kidney beans, drained and rinsed	3	tablespoons finely chopped fresh parsley
1	cup (200 g) canned white kidney beans, drained and rinsed	2	cups (100 g) mixed salad greens
1¼	cups (250 g) canned tuna, drained and flaked	¼	cup (60 ml) freshly squeezed lemon juice
2	stalks celery, thinly sliced		Salt and freshly ground black pepper
1	cucumber, peeled and diced	1	tablespoon snipped fresh chives

1. **Combine** the beans, tuna, celery, cucumber, parsley, salad greens, and lemon juice in a large bowl. Season with salt and pepper and toss gently.

2. **Spoon** into bowls, sprinkle with the chives, and serve.

AMOUNT PER SERVING	191	21g	6g	6g	15g	1.1g
NUTRITION FACTS	**CALORIES**	**PROTEIN**	**FAT**	**FIBER**	**CARBS**	**SALT**
PERCENT DAILY VALUES (based on 2000 calories)	9%	46%	7%	24%	12%	18%

If you liked this recipe, you will love these as well.

marinated bean salad

98

quinoa, corn & pinto bean salad

128

tuna pasta salad

224

fresh salmon salad
with pine nuts

Salmon is one of nature's superfoods. It is rich in protein and omega-3 fatty acids, as well as vitamin D, several B vitamins, and selenium. It is also easy to cook and is liked by most people, even those who are not normally fond of fish.

Serves 4

10 minutes

6–8 minutes

2

1/3	cup (90 ml) extra-virgin olive oil
3	tablespoons freshly squeezed lime juice
1	clove garlic, finely chopped
2	(8-ounce/250-g) fresh salmon fillets
4	stalks celery, sliced

20	cherry tomatoes, halved
1	small onion, thinly sliced
2	tablespoons snipped fresh chives
	Salt and freshly ground black pepper
1/4	cup (30 g) pine nuts, toasted

1. **Heat** the oil in a medium frying pan over medium heat. Stir in 2 tablespoons of lime juice and the garlic and simmer for 1 minute.

2. **Add** the salmon and cook until the fish flakes easily when tested with a fork, about 3 minutes on each side.

3. **Transfer** the salmon to a plate and let cool a little. Reserve the pan juices in a small bowl.

4. **Divide** the celery, tomatoes, and onion evenly among four individual serving plates.

5. **Gently flake** the salmon, discarding any skin and bones. Add to the salads and sprinkle with the chives.

6. **Add** the remaining lime juice to the bowl with the reserved pan juices and season with salt and pepper.

7. **Spoon** some of the cooking juice mixture over each salad. Sprinkle with the pine nuts and serve.

AMOUNT PER SERVING	370	15g	33g	2g	4g	0.1g
NUTRITION FACTS	**CALORIES**	**PROTEIN**	**FAT**	**FIBER**	**CARBS**	**SALT**
PERCENT DAILY VALUES (based on 2000 calories)	18%	33%	41%	8%	3%	2%

If you liked this recipe, you will love these as well.

apple, nut & celery salad

40

papaya, avocado & salmon salad

204

salmon & lentil salad

212

bread salad with poached trout

Dark green "ridge" cucumbers are sometimes called Lebanese cucumbers. If unavailable, substitute the ordinary variety.

Serves 4

15 minutes

12 minutes

1

TROUT

4	fresh trout fillets, skinned and boned
10	small sprigs fresh rosemary
	Salt and freshly ground black pepper
2	lemons; 1 thinly sliced, 1 juiced
1/2	cup (125 ml) dry white wine
2	tablespoons balsamic vinegar
1	tablespoon extra-virgin olive oil

BREAD SALAD

4	slices crusty bread
2	tablespoons extra-virgin olive oil
2	tablespoons freshly grated Parmesan cheese
3	plum or vine-ripened tomatoes, diced
1	Lebanese cucumber, with peel, cut in large dice
1	small red onion, diced
1/2	cup (50 g) black olives
1	red bell pepper (capsicum), diced
1	tablespoon capers, rinsed
3	tablespoons finely chopped fresh basil

1. **To prepare the trout,** place in a large frying pan. Top with the rosemary and season with salt and pepper. Cover with the lemon slices.

2. **Pour** in the wine and lemon juice. Cover the pan and poach the trout over medium heat until the flesh is opaque, about 4 minutes. Remove the trout from the pan and set aside.

3. **Whisk** the vinegar and oil in a small bowl. Set aside.

4. **To prepare the bread salad,** preheat the broiler (grill) to medium. Toast the bread until lightly browned on one side, 3–4 minutes. Turn over. Brush the other side with oil. Sprinkle with the Parmesan. Broil until the cheese is melted and golden, 2–3 minutes. Cut into 1-inch (2.5-cm) squares to make cheese croutons.

5. **Combine** the croutons, tomatoes, cucumbers, onion, olives, bell pepper, capers, and basil in a large bowl. Toss to combine.

6. **To serve,** divide the salad among four serving plates. Top each one with a fish fillet and drizzle with the oil and vinegar mixture.

AMOUNT PER SERVING	361 CALORIES	32g PROTEIN	16g FAT	2g FIBER	21g CARBS	1.3g SALT
NUTRITION FACTS	17%	70%	20%	8%	16%	22%
PERCENT DAILY VALUES (based on 2000 calories)						

jumbo shrimp salad

If you have raw shrimp, you can cook it for this recipe by simmering it in lightly salted boiling water (or fish or vegetable stock) until it turns pink, 2–3 minutes.

Serves 6

10 minutes

1

SALAD

1	iceberg lettuce, leaves torn
1	onion, sliced
28	cherry tomatoes, halved
2	carrots, quartered lengthwise, then sliced
2	red bell peppers (capsicums), cut into thin strips
40	peeled, cooked jumbo shrimps (king prawns), deveined, tails intact
2	tablespoons finely chopped fresh parsley

DRESSING

1/3	cup (90 ml) extra-virgin olive oil
1/4	cup (60 ml) freshly squeezed lemon juice
1/2	teaspoon Thai sweet chili sauce
	Freshly ground black pepper

1. **To prepare the salad,** arrange the lettuce in a shallow salad bowl. Top with the onion, cherry tomatoes, carrots, bell peppers, shrimp, and parsley.

2. **Whisk** the oil, lemon juice, and chili sauce in a small bowl. Season with the pepper.

3. **Drizzle** over the salad and serve.

AMOUNT PER SERVING	423	10g	5g	2g	8g	0.2g
NUTRITION FACTS	CALORIES	PROTEIN	FAT	FIBER	CARBS	SALT
PERCENT DAILY VALUES (based on 2 000 calories)	20%	22%	6%	8%	6%	4%

If you liked this recipe, you will love these as well.

gilled baby octopus salad

186

shrimp salad with avocados

188

mixed seafood salad

202

mediterranean seafood salad

Precooked seafood mixes are available from delicatessens and in the freezer or refrigerated sections of most supermarkets. If desired, use a 1-pound (500-g) package of frozen mixed seafood and cook according to the instructions on the package.

 Serves 4

15 minutes

 1

DRESSING

2	tablespoons Dijon mustard Juice and finely grated zest of 2 limes
5	tablespoons thick, creamy Greek-style yogurt
3	tablespoons tomato ketchup
1	small red chile, seeded and finely chopped
¼	cup (60 ml) extra-virgin olive oil
3	tablespoons finely chopped fresh dill or mint
	Salt

SALAD

1	romaine (cos) lettuce, coarsely chopped
1	pound (500 g) precooked mixed seafood (shrimp, calamari, mussels, scallops, etc.), thawed if frozen
2	large red onions, chopped

1. **To prepare the dressing,** mix the mustard, lime juice, yogurt, ketchup, and chile in a medium bowl.

2. **Whisk** in the oil, a little at a time, then stir in the dill or mint and lime zest. Season with salt.

3. **To assemble the salad,** put the lettuce in a salad bowl and top with the seafood and onions. Drizzle with the dressing and serve.

AMOUNT PER SERVING NUTRITION FACTS PERCENT DAILY VALUES (based on 2000 calories)	344 CALORIES 17%	27g PROTEIN 59%	21g FAT 26%	3g FIBER 12%	13g CARBS 10%	1.6g SALT 27%

If you liked this recipe, you will love these as well.

mixed seafood salad

202

shrimp & scallop salad

208

mixed seafood salad

Soak the mussels in cold water for one hour, then scrub off any beards with a wire brush. If you have raw shrimp, simmer in lightly salted boiling water until pink, 2–3 minutes.

Serves 6

25 minutes

4 hours

10–15 minutes

2

16 ounces (400 g) mussels, in shell

2 cups (500 ml) dry white wine

8 ounces (250 g) scallops, shucked

5 ounces (150 g) squid, cut into rings

8 ounces (250 g) peeled cooked shrimp (prawns), deveined

⅓ cup (90 ml) extra-virgin olive oil

2 tablespoons freshly squeezed lemon juice

1 tablespoon snipped fresh chives

1 tablespoon fresh cilantro (coriander) leaves

Salt

1. **Combine** the mussels and wine in a large saucepan. Cover, bring to a boil, and simmer until the shells open, 5–10 minutes. Discard any that do not open. Remove the mussels with a slotted spoon and place in a large bowl.

2. **Add** the scallops and squid to the saucepan. Simmer over medium heat for 2 minutes.

3. **Remove** with a slotted spoon and add to the mussels. Let cool slightly, then add the shrimp.

4. **Whisk** the oil, lemon juice, chives, cilantro, and salt in a small bowl. Drizzle over the salad.

5. **Toss lightly** and chill in the refrigerator for four hours before serving.

AMOUNT PER SERVING	281 CALORIES	25g PROTEIN	16g FAT	0g FIBER	3g CARBS	0.6g SALT
NUTRITION FACTS						
PERCENT DAILY VALUES (based on 2 000 calories)	14%	54%	20%	0%	2%	10%

If you liked this recipe, you will love these as well.

crab salad with fennel
190

mediterranean seafood salad
200

papaya, avocado & salmon salad

The sweet yellow flesh of the papaya, or papaw as it is know in some parts of the world, is the perfect partner to the creamy avocados and delicately flavored pink salmon.

Serves 4

20 minutes

1

SALAD
- 1 papaya, halved
- 2 avocados, pitted and cut into cubes
- 1 tablespoon freshly squeezed lemon juice
- 2 (7-ounce/200-g) cans pink salmon
- 2 cups (100 g) mixed salad greens

PAPAYA SEED DRESSING
- 1/3 cup (90 ml) extra-virgin olive oil
- 1/4 cup (60 ml) white vinegar
- 1 scallion (spring onion), chopped
- 2 teaspoons sugar
- 1/2 teaspoon salt
- 1 teaspoon Dijon mustard
- Reserved papaya seeds

1. **To prepare the salad,** remove the seeds from the papaya, reserving one tablespoon for the dressing. Peel and cut the flesh into cubes.

2. **Put** the avocado in a shallow bowl and drizzle with the lemon juice.

3. **Drain** the salmon, remove any bones, and break into chunks.

4. **Arrange** the salad greens in four individual serving dishes.

5. **Gently toss** the avocado, salmon, and papaya in a medium bowl and arrange on the salad greens.

6. **To prepare the dressing,** place the oil, vinegar, scallion, sugar, salt, mustard, and papaya seeds in a food processor. Process until the seeds look like freshly ground black pepper.

7. **Drizzle** the dressing over the salads and serve.

 AMOUNT PER SERVING / **NUTRITION FACTS** / **PERCENT DAILY VALUES** (based on 2 000 calories)

 470 CALORIES 23%

 21g PROTEIN 46%

 41g FAT 51%

 3g FIBER 12%

 6g CARBS 5%

1.6g SALT 26%

shrimp & mango salad

If you have raw shrimp, simmer them in lightly salted boiling water (or fish or vegetable stock) until pink, 2–3 minutes.

 Serves 4

 20 minutes

 1

SALAD

1   (14-ounce/400-g) can mangoes in juice
2   scallions (spring onions), sliced on the diagonal
8   ounces (250 g) cooked shrimp (prawns), peeled and deveined
    Baby spinach leaves

DRESSING

½   cup (125 ml) plain yogurt
¼   cup (60 ml) mango chutney
¼   cup (60 ml) reserved mango juice

1. **To prepare the salad,** drain the mangoes, reserving ¼ cup (60 ml) of juice. Cut the mangoes into thin slices.

2. **Mix** the mangoes, scallions, and shrimp in a medium bowl.

3. **Arrange** the spinach leaves on four individual serving plates. Top with the shrimp mixture.

4. **To prepare the dressing,** whisk the yogurt, mango chutney, and reserved mango juice in a medium bowl until well combined.

5. **Drizzle** the dressing over the salads and serve.

AMOUNT PER SERVING	150	13g	1g	2g	21g	1g
NUTRITION FACTS	**CALORIES**	**PROTEIN**	**FAT**	**FIBER**	**CARBS**	**SALT**
PERCENT DAILY VALUES (based on 2 000 calories)	7%	28%	1%	8%	16%	16%

If you liked this recipe, you will love these as well.

papaya, avocado & salmon salad

204

thai calamari salad

216

shrimp & scallop salad

Scallops spoil very quickly and for this reason they are usually shucked and gutted immediately after harvest. What's left is the large white muscle.

 Serves 8

 20 minutes

2 hours

5 minutes

2

DRESSING

- ½ cup (125 ml) extra-virgin olive oil
- ¼ cup (60 ml) freshly squeezed lemon juice
- 2 tablespoons finely chopped fresh parsley
- 2 tablespoons finely chopped fresh basil
  Salt and freshly ground black pepper

SALAD

- 1 pound (500 g) raw shrimp (prawns), shelled (tails intact) and deveined
- 1 tablespoon extra-virgin olive oil
- 1 pound (500 g) scallops
- 2 stalks celery, sliced
- 12 stuffed green olives, halved
- 1 romaine (cos) lettuce, torn

1. **To prepare the dressing,** whisk the oil, lemon juice, parsley, basil, salt, and pepper in a small bowl.

2. **To prepare the salad,** bring a medium saucepan of salted water to a boil. Add the shrimp and cover the pan. When the water returns to a boil, simmer the shrimp until pink, 2–3 minutes

3. **Using** a slotted spoon, transfer the shrimp to a colander. Refresh under cold running water, drain again, and dry on a clean kitchen towel.

4. **Heat** the oil in a medium saucepan over medium-high heat. Add the scallops and sauté until tender and cooked through, 2–4 minutes. Set aside to cool.

5. **Combine** the shrimp, scallops, celery, and olives in a medium bowl. Drizzle with the dressing and toss gently. Cover the bowl and chill in the refrigerator for 2 hours.

6. **Arrange** the lettuce leaves in a shallow salad bowl. Pile the shrimp and scallop mixture on top and serve.

AMOUNT PER SERVING	379	35g	24g	1g	4g	0.8g
NUTRITION FACTS	CALORIES	PROTEIN	FAT	FIBER	CARBS	SALT
PERCENT DAILY VALUES (based on 2000 calories)	18%	76%	30%	4%	3%	13%

If you liked this recipe, you will love these as well.

shrimp & mango salad

206

seared scallop salad

214

shrimp salad with roasted pecan dressing

If you can't find roasted pecans, make your own. Roast 1 cup (125 g) of shelled pecans in 2 tablespoons of butter in a slow oven (250°F/105°C), stirring occasionally, for 50–60 minutes.

 Serves 4

 20 minutes

 1

SALAD

1	avocado, peeled, pitted, and cut into chunks
2	hard-boiled eggs, quartered
8	button mushrooms, sliced
16	cooked, shelled (tail intact) shrimp (prawns)
1	cup (50 g) mixed salad greens

ROAST PECAN DRESSING

1	cup (125 g) roasted pecans
5	tablespoons (75 ml) extra-virgin olive oil
¼	cup (60 ml) white vinegar
2	teaspoons Dijon mustard
1	teaspoon sugar

1. **To prepare the salad,** put the avocado in a large serving bowl. Add the eggs and mushrooms, followed by the shrimp, and salad greens.

2. **To prepare the roast pecan dressing,** combine the pecans, oil, vinegar, mustard, and sugar in a food processor and process until smooth.

3. **Spoon** the dressing over the salad and serve.

AMOUNT PER SERVING	315	8g	30g	2g	2g	1.7g
NUTRITION FACTS	CALORIES	PROTEIN	FAT	FIBER	CARBS	SALT
PERCENT DAILY VALUES (based on 2000 calories)	15%	17%	37%	6%	2%	28%

If you liked this recipe, you will love these as well.

shrimp salad with avocados

188

mediterranean seafood salad

200

salmon & lentil salad

If you are short on time, use well-drained canned lentils in this salad. Otherwise, simmer ½ cup (100 g) of dried green lentils and ½ cup (100 g) dried red lentils over low heat until tender, about 30 minutes. Drain and let cool.

Serves 4

15 minutes

5 minutes

1

DRESSING

1	cup (250 ml) mayonnaise
2	tablespoons vegetable stock
1	tablespoon whole-grain mustard
1	tablespoon white wine vinegar

SALAD

1	romaine (cos) lettuce, leaves separated and torn into large pieces
½	cup (100 g) dried green lentils, drained
½	cup (100 g) dried red lentils, drained
20	cherry tomatoes, halved
5	ounces (150 g) whole-wheat (wholemeal) croûtons
1	tablespoon chile oil or extra-virgin olive oil
14	ounces (400 g) salmon fillets, skin removed, cut into 1-inch (2.5-cm) pieces
1	ounce (30 g) Parmesan cheese shavings
	Salt and freshly ground black pepper

1. **To prepare the dressing,** whisk the mayonnaise, vegetable stock, mustard, and vinegar in a medium bowl. Chill in the refrigerator until ready to use.

2. **To prepare the salad,** cook the lentils together in salted boiling water until tender, about 30 minutes. Drain and rinse under cold running water. Drain again and set aside.

3. **Combine** the lettuce, lentils, tomatoes, and croûtons on a large serving platter.

4. **Heat** the oil in a large frying pan over medium heat. Add the salmon and cook, turning several times, until tender, about 4 minutes. Break the salmon into pieces with a fork. Arrange on top of the salad.

5. **Drizzle** the dressing over the salad and top with the Parmesan. Season with salt and pepper and serve.

AMOUNT PER SERVING	659	34g	69g	5g	40g	1.5g
NUTRITION FACTS	**CALORIES**	**PROTEIN**	**FAT**	**FIBER**	**CARBS**	**SALT**
PERCENT DAILY VALUES (based on 2000 calories)	32%	74%	85%	20%	31%	26%

If you liked this recipe, you will love these as well.

warm potato & salmon salad

220

spiced chicken and dhal salad

238

seared scallop salad

It is important not to overcook scallops. For small scallops like the ones in this salad, 2–3 minutes in a hot pan will be enough.

 Serves 4

 10 minutes

 6–8 minutes

 2

MUSTARD DRESSING

5	tablespoons mayonnaise
2	tablespoon extra-virgin olive oil
1	teaspoon sesame oil
1	tablespoon white wine vinegar
2	teaspoons Dijon mustard

SALAD

2	tablespoon extra-virgin olive oil
3	cloves garlic, finely chopped
1	pound (500 g) bay scallops
6	slices bacon, rinds removed, chopped
1	romaine (cos) lettuce, leaves separated, torn
2	ounces (60 g) croûtons
2	ounces (60 g) Parmesan cheese, shaved

1. **To prepare the mustard dressing,** whisk the mayonnaise, olive oil, sesame oil, vinegar, and mustard in a medium bowl. Set aside.

2. **To prepare the salad,** heat the oil in a large frying pan over high heat. Add the garlic and scallops and sauté until the scallops are tender and cooked through, 2–4 minutes. Remove from the pan and set aside.

3. **Put** the bacon in the same pan over medium heat and sauté until crisp and golden, about 5 minutes. Drain on paper towels.

4. **Put** the lettuce leaves in a large salad bowl. Add the half dressing and toss to coat. Add the bacon, croûtons, and shavings of Parmesan cheese and toss to combine. Spoon the scallop mixture over the top, drizzle with the remaining dressing, and serve.

AMOUNT PER SERVING	613	42g	42g	2g	17g	2.6g
NUTRITION FACTS	**CALORIES**	**PROTEIN**	**FAT**	**FIBER**	**CARBS**	**SALT**
PERCENT DAILY VALUES (based on 2 000 calories)	29%	91%	52%	8%	13%	44%

If you liked this recipe, you will love these as well.

shrimp & mango salad

206

shrimp & scallop salad

208

thai calamari salad

Thai basil has a pronounced licorice or anise flavor. Because of this, it is sometimes called anise or licorice basil. Its leaves are deep green and smaller than the regular variety.

Serves 4

30 minutes

20 minutes

5 minutes

3

SALAD

4 calamari tubes, cleaned
6 ounces (180 g) green beans, sliced lengthwise
2 tomatoes, cut into wedges
1 small green papaya, peeled, seeded, and shredded
4 scallions (spring onions) sliced
3 tablespoons finely chopped fresh cilantro (coriander)
3 tablespoons finely chopped fresh Thai basil
1 fresh red chile, seeded and chopped

LIME DRESSING

2 teaspoons brown sugar
3 tablespoons freshly squeezed lime juice
1 tablespoon Thai fish sauce

1. **To prepare the salad,** make a single cut down the length of each calamari tube with a sharp knife and open out. Cut parallel lines down the length of the calamari, taking care not to cut through the flesh. Makecuts in the opposite direction to form a cubed pattern.

2. **Heat** a nonstick grill pan or frying pan over high heat. Add the calamari and cook until the flesh is just tender, 2–3 minutes in all.

3. **Remove** from the pan, let cool slightly, then cut into chunks.

4. **Blanch** the green beans in salted boiling water for 1 minute. Drain and refresh until cold running water. Drain again thoroughly.

5. **Combine** the calamari, green beans, tomatoes, papaya, scallions, cilantro, basil, and chile in a large serving bowl.

6. **To prepare the dressing,** whisk the sugar, lime juice, and fish sauce in a small bowl.

7. **Drizzle** the dressing over the salad and toss to combine. Cover and let stand for 20 minutes before serving.

AMOUNT PER SERVING	100	15g	1g	5g	7g	1.2g
NUTRITION FACTS	CALORIES	PROTEIN	FAT	FIBER	CARBS	SALT
PERCENT DAILY VALUES (based on 2000 calories)	5%	33%	1%	20%	5%	21%

If you liked this recipe, you will love these as well.

thai rice salad

160

thai beef salad

270

thai fish & mango salad

Thai fish sauce, or *nam pla*, is made of fermented small, whole fish (or shrimp) and is quite salty, so a little goes a long way.

 Serves 4

 25 minutes

 3–5 minutes

2

2	small mangoes, peeled and sliced
2	small cucumbers, with peel, thinly sliced
1	red bell pepper (capsicum), cut into thin strips
2	tablespoons fresh mint sprigs
2	tablespoons fresh cilantro (coriander) leaves
⅓	cup (90 ml) freshly squeezed lime juice
1	teaspoon fresh ginger, grated

2	tablespoons Thai fish sauce
2	tablespoons Thai sweet chili sauce
1	tablespoon grated light palm sugar or light brown sugar
4	medium fillets firm-textured white fish
2	tablespoons peanut oil
3	tablespoons unsalted peanuts, coarsely chopped

1. **Combine** the mangoes, cucumbers, bell pepper, mint, and cilantro in a salad bowl. Toss well, cover, and refrigerate.

2. **Whisk** the lime juice, ginger, fish sauce, sweet chili sauce, and palm sugar in a small bowl.

3. **Preheat** a grill pan on high heat. Brush the fish fillets with the peanut oil and grill until cooked, 3–5 minutes.

4. **Add** the fish fillets to the salad bowl. Drizzle with the lime mixture. Sprinkle with the peanuts and serve.

AMOUNT PER SERVING	178	23g	2g	2g	18g	1.9g
NUTRITION FACTS	**CALORIES**	**PROTEIN**	**FAT**	**FIBER**	**CARBS**	**SALT**
PERCENT DAILY VALUES (based on 2 000 calories)	9%	50%	2%	8%	14%	31%

If you liked this recipe, you will love these as well.

papaya, avocado & salmon salad

204

shrimp & mango salad

206

warm potato & salmon salad

This is a hearty salmon dish and can be served as a complete meal in itself.

 Serves 4

 30 minutes

 45 minutes

 1

SALAD

1	pound (500 g) salmon fillet, skin removed and cut into large cubes
1	pound (500 g) baby (new) potatoes, halved
	Olive oil cooking spray
12	baby corn (sweet corn)
3	ounces (90 g) sun-dried tomatoes, drained

DRESSING

½	cup (120 ml) plain yogurt
3	tablespoons Thai sweet chili sauce
2	tablespoons freshly squeezed lemon juice

1. **Preheat** the oven to 400°F (200°C/gas 6). Put the potatoes in a large baking dish and lightly spray with oil. Roast for 30 minutes, turning a couple of times during cooking. Add the baby corn to the potatoes and roast until both vegetables are tender, about 10 more minutes. Set aside.

2. **Lightly spray** a grill pan with oil and grill the salmon cubes over high heat until just tender and golden, 3–4 minutes.

3. **To prepare the dressing**, whisk the yogurt, sweet chili sauce, and lemon juice in a small bowl.

4. **Combine** the potatoes, baby corn, and dried tomatoes in a medium bowl and toss.

5. **Arrange** the potato salad mixture on individual plates. Top with the salmon, drizzle with the dressing, and serve.

AMOUNT PER SERVING	435	29g	24g	2g	27g	1.8g
NUTRITION FACTS	CALORIES	PROTEIN	FAT	FIBER	CARBS	SALT
PERCENT DAILY VALUES (based on 2 000 calories)	21%	63%	30%	8%	21%	31%

If you liked this recipe, you will love these as well.

artichoke & potato salad with lemon mayonnaise

172

potato salad with bacon

176

grilled potato salad

178

pickled daikon noodle salad
with shrimp

Daikon is a large, mild-flavored radish used in Japanese cooking. It is available in Asian food stores and from online suppliers.

 Serves 4

15 minutes

5 minutes

 1

14 ounces (400 g) dried cellophane noodles

12 ounces (350 g) cooked shrimp (prawns), peeled and deveined

1 (3-inch/7.5-cm) piece pickled daikon, julienned

5 ounces (150 g) snow peas (mangetout), very thinly sliced

2 tablespoons sesame oil

1. **Cook** the noodles according to the instructions on the package.

2. **Drain well** and transfer to a large bowl.

3. **Add** the shrimp, daikon, snow peas, and sesame oil.

4. **Toss well** and serve.

AMOUNT PER SERVING	442	25g	11g	4g	63g	0.4g
NUTRITION FACTS	CALORIES	PROTEIN	FAT	FIBER	CARBS	SALT
PERCENT DAILY VALUES (based on 2 000 calories)	21%	54%	14%	16%	48%	7%

If you liked this recipe, you will love these as well.

rice noodle salad

134

thai noodle salad

136

tuna pasta salad

If desired, replace the canned tuna with two 6-ounce (180-g) fresh tuna steaks. Drizzle with oil, season with salt and pepper, and grill in a hot grill pan until tender, 3–4 minutes on each side. Crumble and add to the pasta.

 Serves 4

 10 minutes

 10–12 minutes

 1

2	(6-ounce/180-g) cans tuna, drained
2	large white onions, finely chopped
3	tablespoons capers, drained
6	tablespoons (90 ml) extra-virgin olive oil

1 pound (500 g) fusilli or other short pasta
Salt and freshly ground black pepper

1. **Combine** the tuna, onions, capers, and 3 tablespoons of oil in a large salad bowl and mix well.

2. **Cook** the pasta in a large pot of salted, boiling water until al dente.

3. **Drain** and cool under cold running water. Drain again and dry on a clean kitchen towel. Add to the salad bowl.

4. **Season** with salt and pepper and drizzle with the remaining 3 tablespoons of oil. Toss well, and serve.

AMOUNT PER SERVING	404 CALORIES	25g PROTEIN	6g FAT	3g FIBER	66g CARBS	0.4g SALT
NUTRITION FACTS PERCENT DAILY VALUES (based on 2000 calories)	19%	54%	7%	12%	51%	6%

If you liked this recipe, you will love these as well.

tuna barley salad

118

mixed beans with tuna

192

Meaty
Business

chicken & potato salad

This is a good way to use up leftover roast chicken or the chicken left over from stock-making. Since they are not cooked, be sure to use only the freshest of in-season zucchini.

 Serves 4

 20 minutes

 2–3 hours

 15–20 minutes

 1

SALAD

8	medium new potatoes, unpeeled
3	cups (500 g) cooked chicken, skin removed, cut into bite-size pieces
2	zucchini (courgettes), coarsely grated
1	teaspoon finely chopped fresh thyme
1	red bell pepper (capsicum), sliced into thin strips
1	tablespoon finely chopped fresh cilantro (coriander)
4	hard-boiled eggs, quartered

DRESSING

1/3	cup (90 ml) extra-virgin olive oil
2	tablespoons freshly squeezed lemon juice
2	tablespoons mayonnaise
	Salt and freshly ground black pepper

1. **To prepare the salad,** cook the potatoes in salted boiling water until tender, 15–20 minutes. Cut into bite-size pieces and let cool.

2. **Combine the chicken,** zucchini, thyme, potatoes, bell pepper, cilantro, and egg in a salad bowl and toss gently.

3. **To prepare the dressing,** whisk the oil, lemon juice, mayonnaise, salt, and pepper in a small bowl. Drizzle over the salad and toss gently.

4. **Chill** in the refrigerator for 2–3 hours before serving.

AMOUNT PER SERVING	601	40g	40g	2g	21g	0.6g
NUTRITION FACTS	**CALORIES**	**PROTEIN**	**FAT**	**FIBER**	**CARBS**	**SALT**
PERCENT DAILY VALUES (based on 2 000 calories)	29%	87%	48%	8%	16%	10%

If you liked this recipe, you will love these as well.

calabrian salad

170

blue cheese potato salad

174

grilled potato salad

178

chicken salad
with parmesan tomatoes

The anchovy paste gives a little extra bite to the dressing without being overpowering.

Serves 4

15 minutes

10 minutes

2

SALAD

4	boneless, skinless chicken breast halves
3	tablespoons extra-virgin olive oil
1	tablespoon finely chopped fresh parsley
1	clove garlic, finely chopped
	Salt and freshly ground black pepper
1	romain 8cos) lettuce heart, torn
1	ounce (30 g) Parmesan cheese, in shavings
16	cherry tomatoes, halved

DRESSING

5	tablespoons (75 ml) extra-virgin olive oil
2	tablespoons freshly squeezed lemon juice
1	tablespoon white wine vinegar
1	teaspoon anchovy paste
1	clove garlic, finely chopped

1. **To prepare the salad,** place the chicken in a single layer in a shallow dish. Whisk the oil, parsley, and garlic in a small bowl. Season with salt and pepper.

2. **Pour** the oil mixture over the chicken. Turn the chicken several times to coat thoroughly. Cover the dish and let stand while you prepare the dressing.

3. **To prepare the dressing,** whisk the oil, lemon juice, vinegar, anchovy paste, and garlic in a small bowl. Set aside.

4. **Heat** a large frying pan over high heat. Add the chicken and marinade and sauté until browned and cooked through, about 10 minutes. Cut into slices about $\frac{1}{2}$-inch (1-cm) thick.

5. **Arrange** the lettuce, Parmesan, and tomatoes in four individual salad bowls. Top with the chicken. Drizzle with the dressing and serve.

AMOUNT PER SERVING	525 CALORIES	31g PROTEIN	34g FAT	1g FIBER	3g CARBS	1.7g SALT
NUTRITION FACTS PERCENT DAILY VALUES (based on 2 000 calories)	25%	67%	42%	5%	2%	28%

If you liked this recipe, you will love these as well.

chicken blue cheese & walnut **salad**

236

chicken salad **with prune vinaigrette**

240

summer salad of grilled chicken, spinach & mango

244

chicken waldorf

You can use the poaching method given in this recipe to cook chicken quickly and easily for all the chicken salads in this chapter.

 Serves 6

 15 minutes

 1 hour

 10–15 minutes

 2

6	boneless, skinless chicken breast halves	2	tablespoons freshly squeezed lemon juice
	Pinch of mixed herbs	2	stalks celery, sliced
	Salt	½	cup (60 g) walnuts, coarsely chopped
2	crisp red apples, cored and cut into bite-size cubes	½	cup (125 ml) mayonnaise

1. **To poach the chicken,** pour 4 cups (1 liter) of water into a medium saucepan. Bring to a boil and add the mixed herbs, salt, and chicken. Simmer until the chicken is cooked, 10–15 minutes. Let sit in the cooking water for 15 minutes. Drain and set aside to cool.

2. **When completely cool,** cut the chicken into bite-size cubes. Drizzle the apples with the lemon juice to prevent them from turning brown.

3. **Combine** the chicken, apples, celery, and walnuts in a large salad bowl. Add the mayonnaise, toss gently, and serve.

AMOUNT PER SERVING	385 CALORIES	29g PROTEIN	28g FAT	1g FIBER	4g CARBS	0.5g SALT
NUTRITION FACTS PERCENT DAILY VALUES (based on 2000 calories)	19%	63%	35%	4%	3%	8%

If you liked this recipe, you will love these as well.

apple, nut & celery **salad**

40

rice salad with apple & walnuts

164

chicken, bean & arugula salad

Like most salad greens, arugula is very low in calories and high in vitamins A and C.
You can use watercress or baby spinach instead.

Serves 4

10 minutes

10 minutes

2

5 tablespoons (75 ml) extra-virgin olive oil

1/3 cup (90 ml) freshly squeezed lemon juice

3 cloves garlic, finely chopped

6 basil leaves, torn

1 tablespoon light brown sugar

Salt and freshly ground black pepper

4 boneless, skinless chicken breast halves

2 cups (500 g) canned white kidney or cannellini beans, rinsed and drained

1 bunch arugula (rocket)

1. **Heat** a grill pan or barbecue on high heat. Whisk the oil, lemon juice, garlic, basil, and sugar in a small bowl. Season with salt and pepper.

2. **Cook** the chicken in the grill pan or barbecue until tender and cooked through, about 10 minutes. Turn the chicken during cooking and baste with two-thirds of the dressing.

3. **Cut** the hot chicken into slices about 1/2-inch (1-cm) thick.

4. **Mix** the beans, arugula, and remaining dressing in a large bowl. Arrange the salad on serving dishes, top with the chicken, and serve while still warm.

AMOUNT PER SERVING	405	32g	24g	4g	18g	0.9g
NUTRITION FACTS	CALORIES	PROTEIN	FAT	FIBER	CARBS	SALT
PERCENT DAILY VALUES (based on 2000 calories)	19%	70%	30%	16%	14%	15%

If you liked this recipe, you will love these as well.

pasta salad with cheese & arugula

148

new mexico chicken salad

246

fennel sausage with zucchini

264

chicken, blue cheese & walnut salad

Blue cheese and walnuts are always a great combo, and in this recipe they really enhance the flavor of the chicken.

Serves 4

15 minutes

45 minutes

10–15 minutes

1

SALAD

4	boneless, skinless chicken breast halves
	Pinch of mixed herbs
	Salt
1	ripe pear, cored and thinly sliced
1	tablespoon freshly squeezed lemon juice
1/2	cup (60 g) walnuts
4	ounces (120 g) blue cheese, crumbled
2	cups (100 g) baby spinach

DRESSING

1/2	cup (125 ml) extra-virgin olive oil
2	tablespoons freshly squeezed lemon juice
1	clove garlic, finely chopped
	Salt and freshly ground black pepper

1. **To prepare the salad,** pour 3 cups (750 ml) of water into a medium saucepan. Bring to a boil and add the mixed herbs, salt, and chicken. Simmer until the chicken is cooked, 10–15 minutes. Let sit in the cooking water for 15 minutes. Drain well and set aside to cool.

2. **Cut** the cooled chicken into 1/2-inch (1-cm) thick slices.

3. **Drizzle** the pear with the lemon juice.

4. **Toss** the chicken, walnuts, pear, blue cheese, and spinach in a salad bowl.

5. **To prepare the dressing,** whisk the oil, lemon juice, garlic, salt, and pepper in a small bowl.

6. **Divide** the salad among four serving dishes. Drizzle with the dressing and serve.

AMOUNT PER SERVING	221	37g	44g	2g	4g	0.9g
NUTRITION FACTS	**CALORIES**	**PROTEIN**	**FAT**	**FIBER**	**CARBS**	**SALT**
PERCENT DAILY VALUES (based on 2000 calories)	11%	80%	54%	7%	3%	15%

If you liked this recipe, you will love these as well.

pear, roquefort & radicchio **salad**

32

chicken salad with parmesan tomatoes

230

spiced chicken & dhal salad

Dhal is a Hindi word for dried and split lentils, as well as a range of spicy legume-based dishes typical of Indian cuisines.

Serves 6

15 minutes

40 minutes

2

8	cups (2 liters) vegetable stock
1½	cups (150 g) green lentils
	Freshly squeezed juice of 2 lemons
2	tablespoons peanut oil
1	tablespoon curry powder
1	tablespoon garam masala
1	teaspoon turmeric
	Salt and freshly ground black pepper
4	boneless, skinless chicken breast halves

1	small cauliflower, cut into florets
1	cup (150 g) frozen peas
2	small tomatoes, diced
1	cucumber, peeled and diced
2	scallions (spring onions), sliced
2	tablespoons finely chopped fresh mint + extra, to garnish
1	bunch watercress

1. **Pour** 6 cups (1.5 liters) of stock into a large saucepan and bring to a boil. Add the lentils and simmer until tender, about 30 minutes.

2. **Drain well** and set aside in a large bowl. Add the lemon juice and 1 tablespoon of the oil. Mix well, cover, and chill in the refrigerator until ready to use.

3. **Combine** the curry powder, garam masala, turmeric, salt, and pepper in a plastic bag. Add the chicken, seal the bag, and shake vigorously so that the spices coat the chicken evenly.

4. **Heat** the remaining 1 tablespoon of oil in a large frying pan over medium-high

heat. Add the chicken and sauté until golden brown and cooked through, about 10 minutes. Set aside.

5. **Pour** the remaining stock into the same pan and bring to a boil. Add the cauliflower and peas and cook over high heat until most of liquid has evaporated.

6. **Add** the cauliflower and pea mixture to the bowl with the lentils and mix well. Stir in the tomatoes, cucumber, scallions, and mint.

7. **Cut** the chicken into ½-inch (1-cm) thick slices and add to the salad. Add the watercress and toss gently. Garnish with the extra mint and serve.

AMOUNT PER SERVING	225	28g	8g	4g	12g	0.8g
NUTRITION FACTS	CALORIES	PROTEIN	FAT	FIBER	CARBS	SALT
PERCENT DAILY VALUES (based on 2000 calories)	11%	61%	10%	16%	9%	13%

chicken salad with prune vinaigrette

Dried prunes are a good source of vitamins A and B6. They are also a natural laxative and are believed to lower the risk of colon cancer and hemorrhoids.

Serves 4

15 minutes

20 minutes

2

SALAD

2	tablespoons extra-virgin olive oil
4	boneless, skinless chicken breast halves
	Salt and freshly ground black pepper
4	ounces (125 g) green beans
2	cups (100 g) baby spinach leaves
1	red onion, thinly sliced
2	tablespoons small capers, drained

PRUNE VINAIGRETTE

12	pitted prunes
½	cup (125 ml) red wine vinegar
1	tablespoon fresh oregano leaves
	Finely grated zest of 1 lemon
1	teaspoon sugar

1. **To prepare the salad,** heat the oil in a large frying pan over high heat. Season the chicken with salt and pepper. Add to the pan and sauté until tender and cooked through, about 10 minutes. Set aside to cool.

2. **Cook** the beans in salted boiling water until crunchy-tender, about 2 minutes.

3. **To prepare the prune vinaigrette,** combine the prunes, vinegar, oregano, lemon zest, and sugar in a small saucepan over low heat. Bring to a boil and simmer for 5 minutes.

4. **Cut** the chicken into ½-inch (1-cm) thick slices. Arrange the spinach, beans, onion, and capers on four serving plates. Top with the chicken.

5. **Drizzle** with the warm dressing and serve immediately.

AMOUNT PER SERVING	278	29g	11g	4g	15g	0.3g
NUTRITION FACTS	**CALORIES**	**PROTEIN**	**FAT**	**FIBER**	**CARBS**	**SALT**
PERCENT DAILY VALUES (based on 2000 calories)	13%	63%	14%	16%	12%	5%

If you liked this recipe, you will love these as well.

summer salad of grilled chicken, spinach and mango
244

chicken waldorf salad with ranch dressing
250

mixed turkey salad with vegetables
254

marinated chicken salad

Warm the honey in the marinade a little, so that it mixes well with the soy sauce and oil.

Serves 6

15 minutes

30 minutes

12 minutes

2

MARINADE

2	tablespoons dark soy sauce
2	tablespoons honey
1	tablespoon sesame oil

SALAD

3	boneless, skinless chicken breast halves, sliced and chopped
2	tablespoons peanut oil
2	tablespoons sesame oil
2	cloves garlic, finely chopped
2	fresh red chiles, seeded and thinly sliced
1	(1-inch/2.5-cm) piece fresh ginger, finely grated
1/3	cup (90 ml) red wine vinegar
1/4	cup (60 ml) water
3	cups (150 g) mixed salad greens

1. **To prepare the marinade,** mix the soy sauce, honey, and sesame oil in a medium glass or ceramic bowl.

2. **Add** the chicken and turn to coat evenly. Cover and chill in the refrigerator for 30 minutes.

3. **Heat** 1 tablespoon of the peanut oil and 1 tablespoon of the sesame oil in a wok or large frying pan over medium heat. Add the chicken and marinade and stir-fry until the chicken is tender and cooked through, 5–6 minutes. Set aside to cool.

4. **Add** the remaining peanut and sesame oils, garlic, chile, and ginger to the pan and stir-fry until the garlic starts to brown, 2–3 minutes.

5. **Stir** in the vinegar and water, bring to a boil, then remove from the heat.

6. **Arrange** the salad greens in a salad bowl and top with the chicken. Drizzle with the warm dressing and serve.

AMOUNT PER SERVING	228	16g	16g	1g	5g	1g
NUTRITION FACTS	**CALORIES**	**PROTEIN**	**FAT**	**FIBER**	**CARBS**	**SALT**
PERCENT DAILY VALUES (based on 2000 calories)	11%	35%	20%	4%	4%	16%

If you liked this recipe, you will love these as well.

pork fillet & apple salad

268

lamb & orange couscous salad

274

lamb salad with herbs

278

summer salad of grilled chicken, spinach & mango

Celebrate the flavors of summer with this superb salad.

Serves 6

1 hour

1–3 hours

2½ hours

3

SALAD

6	tomatoes, halved lengthwise
10	fresh basil leaves, chopped
10	fresh mint leaves, chopped
	Salt and freshly ground black pepper
½	teaspoon sugar
2	tablespoons sesame oil
4	boneless, skinless chicken breast halves
1	bunch asparagus
2	cups (100 g) baby spinach
4	scallions (spring onions), sliced
8	button mushrooms, sliced
2	mangoes, peeled and diced
1	avocado, peeled and diced
½	cup (60 g) toasted hazelnuts
½	cup (60 g) toasted brazil nuts, lightly crushed
½	cup (60 g) toasted pistachios, lightly crushed

DRESSING

3	tablespoons raspberry vinegar
2	tablespoons balsamic vinegar
2	tablespoons light soy sauce
2	teaspoons Dijon mustard
2	teaspoons honey
1	inch (2.5-cm) piece ginger, finely chopped
2	cloves garlic, finely chopped
1	teaspoon chile paste
2	tablespoons freshly squeezed lemon juice
2	tablespoons extra-virgin olive oil

1. **Preheat** the oven to 450°F (220°C/gas 8). Season the tomatoes with the basil, mint, salt, pepper, and sugar. Grease a large baking dish with the oil and arrange the tomatoes cut-side up in a single layer. Roast for 15 minutes. Reduce the oven temperature to 300°F (150°C/gas 2) and roast until they have shrivelled to about half their original size, about 1½ hours. Let cool.

2. **To prepare the dressing,** whisk all the ingredients in a small bowl.

3. **Place** the chicken in a large glass or ceramic bowl. Add ½ cup (125 ml) of the dressing and marinate for 2 hours.

4. **Heat** a grill pan on high heat. Drain the chicken, reserving the marinade, and grill until tender and cooked, 4–5 minutes each side. Baste with the marinade. Set aside and keep warm.

5. **Steam** the asparagus until tender, then refresh under cold water. Drain well.

6. **To assemble the salad,** put the spinach in a large bowl and add the asparagus, scallions, mushrooms, and roasted tomatoes. Add the remaining dressing and toss gently. Divide the salad among six serving plates. Top with mango and avocado cubes. Cover with the chicken and nuts and serve.

AMOUNT PER SERVING						
NUTRITION FACTS	458 CALORIES	28g PROTEIN	36g FAT	4g FIBER	6g CARBS	1.1g SALT
PERCENT DAILY VALUES (based on 2000 calories)	22%	61%	44%	16%	5%	19%

new mexican chicken salad

The availability of edible flowers depends on the season, but zucchini, chervil, basil, and garlic flowers are the most common. Do not eat flowers that are not marketed as edible and make sure they have not been treated with pesticides.

 Serves 4

 10 minutes

 1

SALAD

1	bunch arugula (rocket)
	Handful of edible flowers of your choice
8	red radicchio leaves, shredded
1	grapefruit, peeled, all white pith removed, segmented
2	smoked chicken breasts, sliced

NUTTY CHILE DRESSING

⅓	cup (90 ml) extra-virgin olive oil
2	tablespoons red wine vinegar
4	tablespoons pine nuts, toasted
2	bay leaves
2	fresh red chiles, seeded and finely chopped
2	tablespoons sugar
	Salt

1. **To prepare the salad,** arrange the arugula, flowers, and radicchio attractively on four serving plates. Top with the grapefruit and chicken.

2. **To prepare the nutty chile dressing,** whisk the oil, vinegar, pine nuts, bay leaves, chiles, sugar, and salt in a small bowl.

3. **Remove** the bay leaves and drizzle the dressing over salad just before serving.

AMOUNT PER SERVING	404	18g	32g	1g	12g	0.1g
NUTRITION FACTS	CALORIES	PROTEIN	FAT	FIBER	CARBS	SALT
PERCENT DAILY VALUES (based on 2000 calories)	19%	39%	40%	4%	9%	2%

If you liked this recipe, you will love these as well.

spicy bean & vegetable salad

104

pasta salad with pickled vegetables & arugula

156

summer salad of grilled chicken, spinach & mango

244

spring chicken salad

Char siu sauce is usually made of a mixture of honey, five-spice powder, fermented tofu, dark soy sauce, hoisin sauce, red food coloring, and sherry or rice wine. It is available in Asian food stores and markets. If preferred, replace with barbecue sauce.

Serves 4

10 minutes

5–10 minutes

2

SALAD

2	tablespoons extra-virgin olive oil
6	boneless, skinless chicken thighs
	Salt and freshly ground black pepper
2	carrots
1	cucumber, with peel
2	scallions (spring onions), sliced on the diagonal
	Handful of snow pea sprouts
	Fresh cilantro (coriander) leaves, to garnish

DRESSING

2	tablespoons char siu sauce
1	tablespoon sesame oil
2	tablespoons finely chopped fresh mint
1/4	cup (60 ml) white wine vinegar

1. **To prepare the salad,** heat the oil in a large frying pan over medium-high heat. Season the chicken with salt and pepper. Add to the pan and sauté until tender and cooked through, 5–10 minutes. Remove from the pan and set aside to cool.

2. **Prepare** the carrots and cucumber by shaving them into paper-thin strips using a potato peeler.

3. **To prepare the dressing,** whisk the char siu sauce, sesame oil, mint, and vinegar in a small bowl.

4. **Combine** the chicken, carrots, cucumber, and scallions in a salad bowl. Drizzle with the dressing and toss gently. Garnish with the snow pea sprouts and cilantro and serve.

AMOUNT PER SERVING	354	36g	21g	1g	4g	0.6g
NUTRITION FACTS	CALORIES	PROTEIN	FAT	FIBER	CARBS	SALT
PERCENT DAILY VALUES (based on 2000 calories)	17%	78%	26%	4%	3%	10%

If you liked this recipe, you will love these as well.

rice noodle salad

134

shrimp & mango salad

206

thai beef salad

270

chicken waldorf salad
with ranch dressing

If pressed for time, use a good-quality commercial brand of ranch dressing. If not, try ours. It makes about 1 cup (250 ml); plenty for this recipe with some left over that will keep in the refrigerator for a few days.

Serves 4

10 minutes

10 minutes

2

SALAD

2 tablespoons extra-virgin olive oil

4 boneless, skinless chicken breast halves

Salt and freshly ground black pepper

2 red apples, cored and sliced

2 tablespoons freshly squeezed lemon juice

2 cups (100 g) watercress

1/3 cup (50 g) walnuts, toasted

RANCH DRESSING

1 small clove garlic, coarsely chopped

1/4 teaspoon salt

1 tablespoon minced red bell pepper (capsicum)

1 tablespoon minced scallion (spring onion), white and green parts

1/2 tablespoon minced shallot

1 teaspoon minced fresh parsley leaves

1/2 teaspoon minced fresh cilantro (coriander) leaves

1/2 teaspoon freshly squeezed lemon juice

Pinch freshly ground black pepper

1/4 cup (60 ml) plain yogurt

1/4 cup (60 ml) mayonnaise

2 tablespoons sour cream

1. **To prepare the salad,** heat the oil in a grill pan over high heat. Season the chicken with salt and pepper. Add to the pan and grill until tender and cooked through, about 10 minutes. Set aside and keep warm.

2. **Put** the apples in a large bowl and drizzle with the lemon juice. Add the watercress and walnuts and toss gently.

3. **Cut** the chicken into 1/2-inch (1-cm) thick slices and add to the salad.

4. **To prepare the ranch dressing,** sprinkle the garlic with the salt and finely chop together.

5. **Mix** the garlic and salt, bell pepper, scallion, shallot, parsley, cilantro, lemon juice, and black pepper together in a medium bowl. Add the yogurt, mayonnaise, and sour cream and whisk until smooth and creamy.

6. **Drizzle** the ranch dressing over the salad and serve.

AMOUNT PER SERVING	468	35g	33g	2g	10g	1g
NUTRITION FACTS	CALORIES	PROTEIN	FAT	FIBER	CARBS	SALT
PERCENT DAILY VALUES (based on 2 000 calories)	22%	76%	41%	8%	8%	16%

warm chicken liver
& pancetta salad

Chicken liver is an excellent source of vitamin A, protein, iron, and phosphorus.
Liver spoils very quickly so always buy and eat the same day.

Serves 4

15 minutes

10 minutes

2

5	tablespoons extra-virgin olive oil	1	tablespoon freshly squeezed lemon juice
8	ounces (250 g) thinly sliced pancetta, coarsely chopped	2	teaspoons whole-grain mustard
2	cloves garlic, finely chopped		Salt
1	pound (500 g) chicken livers, halved	2	cups (100 g) baby spinach leaves

1. **Heat** 1 tablespoon oil in a frying pan over medium-high heat. Sauté the pancetta until crisp and golden, about 5 minutes. Drain on paper towels.

2. **Heat** 2 tablespoons of the remaining oil in the same pan over high heat. Add the garlic and chicken livers and sauté until the livers are browned and cooked through, about 5 minutes.

3. **Whisk** the lemon juice, remaining 2 tablespoons of oil, mustard, and salt in a small bowl.

4. **Arrange** the spinach on four serving plates. Top with the chicken livers and pancetta, drizzle with the dressing, and serve.

AMOUNT PER SERVING	314	35g	19g	1g	1g	2.2g
NUTRITION FACTS	**CALORIES**	**PROTEIN**	**FAT**	**FIBER**	**CARBS**	**SALT**
PERCENT DAILY VALUES (based on 2 000 calories)	15%	76%	23%	4%	1%	36%

If you liked this recipe, you will love these as well.

melon zucchini & pancetta **salad**

28

wild salad greens with pancetta & balsamic vinegar

44

sautéed duck salad with thyme & honey

256

mixed turkey salad
with vegetables

Vary the vegetables in this recipe according to what you like or have on hand.
You may also replace the turkey ham with ordinary ham.

Serves 6

5 minutes

1 hour

3–5 minutes

2

SALAD

5	ounces (150 g) green beans, sliced
4	carrots, cut into ½-inch (1-cm) diagonal slices
1	small head broccoli, divided into florets
1	cup (150 g) frozen peas
4	scallions (spring onions), sliced
6	canned artichoke hearts, drained and halved
6	mushrooms, sliced
12	ounces (375 g) sliced turkey ham
12	cherry tomatoes, halved

VINAIGRETTE

⅓	cup (90 ml) extra-virgin olive oil
2	tablespoons freshly squeezed lemon juice
1	teaspoon Dijon mustard Salt and freshly ground white pepper

1. **To prepare the salad,** cook the green beans, carrots, broccoli, and peas in salted boiling water until crunchy-tender, 3–5 minutes. Drain well and set aside to cool.

2. **Combine** the cooked vegetables, scallions, artichokes, and mushrooms in a medium salad bowl.

3. **To prepare the vinaigrette,** whisk the oil, lemon juice, mustard, salt, and white pepper in a small bowl.

4. **Drizzle** the vinaigrette over the vegetables in the bowl and toss gently. Cover and chill in the refrigerator for 1 hour.

5. **Add** the turkey ham and tomatoes, toss gently, and serve.

AMOUNT PER SERVING	245 CALORIES	19g PROTEIN	6g FAT	3g FIBER	9g CARBS	1.2g SALT
NUTRITION FACTS PERCENT DAILY VALUES (based on 2 000 calories)	12%	41%	7%	12%	7%	20%

If you liked this recipe, you will love these as well.

orange & artichoke salad

36

bean salad with artichokes

84

eggplant salad with prosciutto

258

sautéed duck salad
with thyme & honey

This is a perfect dish for special occasions and can be prepared well in advance of eating.

 Serves 4

 25 minutes

 15–20 minutes

 3

2	duck breasts, skin on
	Salt and freshly ground black pepper
1	tablespoon peanut oil
1	teaspoon butter
1	sprig thyme, leaves picked from the stalk
2	tablespoons honey

1	tablespoon freshly squeezed lemon juice
2	tablespoons walnut oil
2	cups (100 g) mixed salad greens
12	cherry tomatoes, halved
	Basil leaves to garnish

1. **Preheat** the oven to 375° F (190°C/gas 5). Season the duck breasts with salt and pepper.

2. **Heat** the peanut oil in a Dutch oven over high heat. Add the duck breasts, skin-side down, and cook until the skin is deep caramel brown.

3. **Transfer** the Dutch oven to the oven and roast the duck until the meat is cooked to your liking; medium-rare will take about 10 minutes.

4. **Discard** the excess fat and put the duck breasts in a bowl.

5. **Heat** the butter in a large frying pan over medium heat until it bubbles. Add the thyme and honey. When simmering, add the duck breasts, skin-side up, and sauté over medium heat until the duck is well coated, 2–3 minutes. Set the duck aside and drain the cooking juices into a small bowl.

6. **Add** the lemon juice, walnut oil, salt, and pepper to the cooking juices and whisk together.

7. **Divide** the salad and tomatoes among four serving plates. Slice the duck breast and place on the salad. Drizzle with the sauce and serve.

AMOUNT PER SERVING	230	17g	15g	1g	8g	0.2g
NUTRITION FACTS	CALORIES	PROTEIN	FAT	FIBER	CARBS	SALT
PERCENT DAILY VALUES (based on 2 000 calories)	11%	37%	19%	4%	6%	4%

If you liked this recipe, you will love these as well.

fresh salmon salad with pine nuts

194

warm chicken liver & pancetta salad

252

lamb salad with herbs

278

eggplant salad with prosciutto

Try to buy ready-sliced prosciutto as it can be quite tricky to do yourself. If you do buy a whole piece, use an electric slicer to get a neat result.

- Serves 4
- 10 minutes
- 1 hour
- 25–30 minutes
- 2

SALAD

2	medium eggplant (aubergine), with peel
	Coarse sea salt
1	cup (150 g) all-purpose (plain) flour
½	cup (125 ml) extra-virgin olive oil
2	cloves garlic, lightly crushed
8	ounces (250 g) prosciutto, thinly sliced
2	hard-boiled eggs, quartered
½	cup (25 g) coarsely chopped salad greens

DRESSING

5	tablespoons (75 ml) extra-virgin olive oil
½	cup (125 ml) sherry or wine vinegar
2	tablespoons lemon juice
2	bay leaves, crumbled
1	tablespoon finely chopped fresh oregano
1	tablespoon finely chopped fresh parsley
	Salt and freshly ground black pepper

1. **To prepare the salad,** cut the eggplant into ½-inch (1-cm) slices. Sprinkle with sea salt and let drain for 30 minutes. Shake the salt off the eggplant. Dredge in the flour.

2. **Heat** half the oil in a large frying pan over medium-high heat. Add the garlic and fry until pale gold. Discard the garlic. Fry the eggplant in 2–3 batches until tender and browned, 5–7 minutes each batch. Drain on paper towels.

3. **Layer** the eggplant and prosciutto on a serving plate. Top with the egg.

4. **To prepare the dressing,** heat the oil, vinegar, lemon juice, bay leaves, oregano, parsley, salt, and pepper in a small saucepan and bring to a boil. Simmer for 5 minutes, the strain.

5. **Drizzle** the dressing over the salad. Let cool, then chill for 30 minutes.

6. **Sprinkle** with the salad greens and serve.

AMOUNT PER SERVING	598	26g	37g	4g	2g	3.1g
NUTRITION FACTS	CALORIES	PROTEIN	FAT	FIBER	CARBS	SALT
PERCENT DAILY VALUES (based on 2 000 calories)	29%	57%	46%	16%	2%	52%

If you liked this recipe, you will love this one as well.

marinated eggplant salad

bacon & egg salad
with frisée

You can whip this salad up in just a few minutes. It makes a great brunch dish for friends and family on weekends.

 Serves 4

10 minutes

10 minutes

1

12	thick slices bacon, rinds removed	4	soft-boiled eggs, halved
2	cups (100 g) cubed bread	¼	cup (60 ml) balsamic vinegar
1	large head frisée lettuce or curly endive leaves		

1. **Sauté** the bacon in a large frying pan over medium heat until crisp and golden, about 5 minutes. Set aside.

2. **Put** the bread in the bacon fat and fry until crisp and golden, about 5 minutes.

3. **Divide** the greens evenly among four serving plates. Top with the eggs, bacon, and fried bread. Drizzle with the balsamic vinegar and serve.

AMOUNT PER SERVING	337	23g	20g	2g	16g	3.6g
NUTRITION FACTS	**CALORIES**	**PROTEIN**	**FAT**	**FIBER**	**CARBS**	**SALT**
PERCENT DAILY VALUES (based on 2000 calories)	16%	50%	25%	8%	12%	60%

If you liked this recipe, you will love these as well.

eggplant salad with prosciutto

258

potato & smoked sausage salad

262

fennel sausage with zucchini

264

potato & smoked sausage
salad

If you're short of time, you can microwave new potatoes. Place in a microwave-proof dish with 2 tablespoons of water. Cover and cook on full power for 5–6 minutes.

Serves 4

20 minutes

40 minutes

2

1	pound (500 g) new potatoes	2	scallions (spring onions), chopped
¼	cup (60 ml) extra-virgin olive oil	1	clove garlic, finely chopped
	Salt	2	teaspoons freshly squeezed lemon juice
2	smoked pork sausages, about 8 ounces (250 g) each, sliced	2	tablespoons snipped fresh chives
1	bunch asparagus, cut into short lengths	⅓	cup (90 ml) plain yogurt
		⅓	cup (90 ml) sour cream

1. **Preheat** the oven to 400°F (200°C/ gas 6). Cut the larger potatoes in half. Bring a large saucepan of water to a boil. Add the potatoes and parboil for 10 minutes. Drain well.

2. **Toss** the potatoes in 2 tablespoon of oil, sprinkle with salt, and spread out in a roasting pan. Roast for 30 minutes until golden brown and crisp, turning occasionally.

3. **Blanch** the asparagus in salted boiling water for 1–2 minutes. Drain well.

4. **Heat** the remaining 2 tablespoons of oil in a large frying pan and sauté the sausages and scallions for 3–4 minutes. Add the asparagus and sauté for 2 more minutes.

5. **Transfer** the sausage mixture to a serving bowl with the roast potatoes.

6. **Whisk** together the garlic, lemon juice, chives, yogurt, and sour cream until smooth. Spoon over the salad and serve warm.

AMOUNT PER SERVING	455	12g	33g	3g	29g	1.4g
NUTRITION FACTS	CALORIES	PROTEIN	FAT	FIBER	CARBS	SALT
PERCENT DAILY VALUES (based on 2000 calories)	22%	26%	41%	12%	22%	24%

If you liked this recipe, you will love these as well.

warm potato & salmon salad

220

chicken & potato salad

228

fennel sausage with zucchini

Select an Italian fennel-flavored sausage for this dish. Substitute with another highly flavored sausage if these are not available.

Serves 4

15 minutes

15 minutes

1

SALAD

⅓	cup (90 ml) extra-virgin olive oil
2	medium zucchini (courgettes), cut into thin slices lengthwise
6	Italian sausages
1	French loaf (baguette), cut in 1-inch (2.5-cm) thick slices
2	cups (100 g) mixed salad greens
2	tablespoons finely chopped basil leaves
4	ounces (125 g) sun-dried tomatoes, packed in oil, drained

DRESSING

3	tablespoons extra-virgin olive oil
3	tablespoons freshly squeezed lemon juice
	Salt and freshly ground black pepper

1. **To prepare the salad,** brush a grill pan with 2 tablespoons of oil and place over medium-high heat. Grill the zucchini, 2–3 minutes each side, then set aside.

2. **Add** the sausages and grill until golden brown, 6–8 minutes. Cut into thick slices.

3. **Brush** the slices of bread with the remaining oil and grill for 2–3 minutes on each side.

4. **Combine** the salad greens, basil, sausages, zucchini, and sun-dried tomatoes in a large serving bowl.

5. **To prepare the dressing,** whisk the oil, lemon juice, salt, and pepper in a small bowl. Drizzle over the salad and serve.

AMOUNT PER SERVING	890	18g	64g	4g	65g	3.4g
NUTRITION FACTS	CALORIES	PROTEIN	FAT	FIBER	CARBS	SALT
PERCENT DAILY VALUES (based on 2000 calories)	43%	39%	79%	16%	50%	56%

roast pork & cherry tomato salad

This is a great way to use up any leftover roast pork. If desired, add a little finely chopped garlic to the dressing and garnish the salad with finely chopped fresh cilantro (coriander).

 Serves 4

10 minutes

 1

SALAD

1	iceberg lettuce, shredded
1	pound (500 g) cold lean roast pork, sliced
1	pound (500 g) cherry tomatoes, halved

DRESSING

⅓	cup (90 ml) extra-virgin olive oil
2	tablespoons white wine vinegar
1	tablespoon whole-grain mustard
	Salt and freshly ground black pepper

1. **To prepare the salad,** arrange the lettuce on four serving plates. Cover with the pork and tomatoes.

2. **To prepare the dressing,** whisk the oil, vinegar, mustard, salt, and pepper in a small bowl.

3. **Drizzle** a little dressing over each salad and serve.

AMOUNT PER SERVING **NUTRITION FACTS** PERCENT DAILY VALUES (based on 2 000 calories)	462 CALORIES 22%	43g PROTEIN 93%	29g FAT 36%	547 FIBER 26%	6g CARBS 5%	0.4g SALT 6%

If you liked this recipe, you will love these as well.

eggplant salad with prosciutto

258

fennel sausage with zucchini

264

pork fillet & apple salad

If desired, grill the apples as well as the pork. Serve the salad as quickly as possible after if has been assembled, before the arugula wilts.

 Serves 4

20 minutes

12 hours

25 minutes

2

SALAD

1	pound (500 g) pork tenderloin
2	tablepoons extra-virgin olive oil
	Salt and freshly ground black pepper
1	tablespoon finely chopped fresh rosemary
1½	cups (150 g) arugula (rocket)
2	crisp red apples, cored and thinly sliced
4	tablespoons Parmesan, in shavings

DRESSING

¼	cup (60 ml) extra-virgin olive oil
2	tablespoons freshly squeezed lemon juice
1	tablespoon Dijon mustard
	Salt and freshly ground black pepper

1. **To prepare the salad,** trim the pork of any sinew and fat and place in a shallow glass or ceramic dish.

2. **Whisk** the oil, salt, pepper, and rosemary in a small bowl and pour over the pork. Turn to coat well. Cover and refrigerate for several hours or overnight.

3. **Heat** a grill pan over medium-high heat. Drain the pork and grill until well cooked, about 10 minutes each side. Remove the pork and cut on the diagonal into ½-inch (1-cm) thick slices.

4. **To prepare the dressing,** whisk the oil, lemon juice, mustard, salt, and pepper in a small bowl.

5. **To assemble the salad,** place the arugula, apples, and Parmesan in a salad bowl. Add the pork and drizzle with the dressing. Toss gently and serve.

AMOUNT PER SERVING	445	31g	33g	1g	8g	0.5g
NUTRITION FACTS	**CALORIES**	**PROTEIN**	**FAT**	**FIBER**	**CARBS**	**SALT**
PERCENT DAILY VALUES (based on 2 000 calories)	21%	67%	41%	2%	6%	9%

If you liked this recipe, you will love these as well.

chicken waldorf salad

232

roast pork & cherry tomato **salad**

266

thai beef salad

Chinese cabbage is a common ingredient in Asian cooking. It has crinkly, thickly veined, cream-colored leaves with green tips. It is crisp and delicately mild in flavor.

Serves 4

30 minutes

10 minutes

 2

1	pound (500 g) boneless rump steak or top round, trimmed
	Salt and freshly ground black pepper
1	small fresh red chile, seeded and finely chopped
2	tablespoons freshly squeezed lime juice
2	tablespoons Thai fish sauce
2	tablespoons grated palm sugar or light brown sugar

1	teaspoon sesame oil
1/4	Chinese or napa cabbage, finely shredded
1/4	cup fresh cilantro (coriander) leaves
1	cup (50 g) fresh mint sprigs
4	ounces (125 g) snow peas (mangetout), trimmed
1	cucumber, thinly sliced
1	small red onion, thinly sliced
16	cherry tomatoes, halved

1. **Heat** a grill pan over medium-high heat. Season the steak with salt and pepper. Grill the steak until cooked to your liking; 5–8 minutes for medium-rare. Remove and slice across the grain.

2. **Whisk** the chile, lime juice, fish sauce, palm sugar, and sesame oil in a small bowl.

3. **Combine** the cabbage, half the cilantro, mint, snow peas, cucumber, onion, and tomatoes on a large serving plate. Top with the steak and drizzle with the dressing. Garnish with the remaining cilantro and serve.

AMOUNT PER SERVING	238	31g	7g	3g	14g	1g
NUTRITION FACTS	CALORIES	PROTEIN	FAT	FIBER	CARBS	SALT
PERCENT DAILY VALUES (based on 2000 calories)	11%	67%	9%	12%	11%	16%

If you liked this recipe, you will love these as well.

thai rice salad
160

thai calamari salad
216

thai fish & mango salad
218

warm steak salad
with papaya & onion

Sweet, fresh papaya goes beautifully with steak. If desired, substitute with sliced fresh mango or peeled diced peaches.

 Serves 4

15 minutes

5 minutes

2

STEAK SALAD

1¼ pounds (600 g) tenderloin (fillet steak), trimmed

1 tablespoon finely chopped fresh rosemary
   Salt

¼ teaspoon cayenne pepper

2 tablespoons butter

1 small papaya, peeled, seeded, and cut into bite-size cubes

1 small red onion, thinly sliced

1 cup (50 g) mixed salad greens

DRESSING

5 tablespoons extra-virgin olive oil

2 tablespoons red wine vinegar
   Salt and freshly ground black pepper

1. **To prepare the steak salad,** cut the steak into thin slices. Sprinkle with the rosemary, salt, and cayenne pepper.

2. **Heat** the butter in a large frying pan over high heat. Add the steak and sauté, tossing gently, until cooked to your liking, 2–5 minutes.

3. **To prepare the dressing,** whisk the vinegar, oil, salt, and pepper in a small bowl.

4. **Mix** the steak, papaya, onion, and greens in a bowl. Drizzle with the dressing and toss well.

5. **Divide** the salad evenly among four serving dishes and serve.

AMOUNT PER SERVING	396	33g	28g	1g	3g	2.9g
NUTRITION FACTS	CALORIES	PROTEIN	FAT	FIBER	CARBS	SALT
PERCENT DAILY VALUES (based on 2000 calories)	19%	72%	35%	4%	2%	48%

If you liked this recipe, you will love these as well.

papaya, avocado & salmon salad

204

shrimp & mango salad

206

thai beef salad

270

lamb & orange couscous salad

Lamb loin is the most tender part of the lamb and requires only very short cooking over high heat.

 Serves 4

20 minutes

4 hours

15 minutes

2

MARINADE

3	tablespoons extra-virgin olive oil
3	tablespoons freshly squeezed lemon juice
2	cloves garlic, finely chopped
1	teaspoon ground cinnamon
1	teaspoon ground allspice or pumpkin pie spice
1	teaspoon honey
1	tablespoon finely chopped fresh oregano
	Salt and freshly ground pepper

COUSCOUS SALAD

1	pound (500 g) lamb loin, trimmed
1	cup (200 g) instant couscous
2	cups (500 ml) chicken stock
1	(14-ounce/400-g) can garbanzo beans (chickpeas), rinsed and drained
12	cherry tomatoes, halved
1	cup (50 g) fresh parsley
1	cup (180 g) raisins
2	oranges, peeled and divided into segments

1. **To prepare the marinade,** whisk the oil, lemon juice, garlic, cinnamon, allspice, honey, oregano, salt, and pepper in a small bowl.

2. **To prepare the salad,** put the lamb in a shallow glass or ceramic bowl. Pour in the marinade, cover, and marinate in the refrigerator for at least 4 hours.

3. **To prepare the couscous salad,** bring the stock to a boil in a medium

pan. Stir in the couscous, remove from the heat, and let cool.

4. **Heat** a grill pan or barbecue over high heat. Drain the lamb and grill until cooked to your liking; about 10 minutes for medium-rare. Let stand for 5 minutes, then cut into $1/2$-inch (1-cm) slices.

5. **Combine** the lamb, garbanzo beans, tomatoes, parsley, raisins, oranges, and couscous in a large bowl and serve.

AMOUNT PER SERVING NUTRITION FACTS *PERCENT DAILY VALUES (based on 2000 calories)	403 CALORIES 19%	32g PROTEIN 70%	29g FAT 36%	1g FIBER 4%	3g CARBS 2%	0.3g SALT 4%

If you liked this recipe, you will love these as well.

couscous with oranges & pistachios

126

lamb salad with herbs

278

barbecued lamb salad

Oyster or phoenix mushrooms are prized for their smooth texture and subtle, oysterlike flavor. If you can't find them, replace with chanterelles or white mushrooms.

 Serves 4

15 minutes

30 minutes

20 minutes

2

1	eggplant (aubergine) Coarse sea salt
4	zucchini (courgettes), cut in quarters lengthwise
¼	cup (60 ml) extra-virgin olive oil
12	oyster (phoenix) mushrooms

¼	cup (60 ml) balsamic vinegar
¼	cup (60 ml) cider vinegar
1	tablespoon honey Salt and freshly ground black pepper
4	noisettes or lamb steaks, cut from the fillet

1. **Cut** the eggplant into ½-inch (1-cm) slices. Sprinkle with sea salt and let drain for 30 minutes. Shake the salt off the eggplant.

2. **Brush** the eggplant and zucchini with oil. Heat a grill pan or barbecue to medium-high and grill until tender, 3–5 minutes. Remove and grill the mushrooms, 2–3 minutes.

3. **Whisk** the balsamic vinegar, cider vinegar, honey, salt, and pepper in a medium bowl.

4. **Dip** the lamb into the vinegar mixture to coat. Grill in the grill pan or on the barbecue until cooked to your liking; 5–8 minutes for medium rare.

5. **Put** the remaining balsamic mixture in a saucepan and bring to a boil. Simmer for 2 minutes.

6. **Arrange** the vegetables and meat on a four individual serving plates. Drizzle the hot vinegar mixture over the top and serve.

AMOUNT PER SERVING NUTRITION FACTS PERCENT DAILY VALUES (based on 2 000 calories)	390 CALORIES 19%	31g PROTEIN 67%	23g FAT 28%	3g FIBER 12%	12g CARBS 9%	0.4g SALT 6%

If you liked this recipe, you will love these as well.

roast pork & cherry tomato salad

266

lamb salad with tzatziki

280

lamb salad with herbs

You can make double the quantities of the marinade and dressing and store in a clean jar in the refrigerator for 2–3 weeks. Both are delicious with green salads.

Serves 6

45 minutes

12 hours

15 minutes

2

ROSEMARY AND LEMON MARINADE

2 tablespoons fresh rosemary leaves

1 teaspoon chopped fresh oregano

1 teaspoon black peppercorns

1 teaspoon finely grated lemon zest

1 tablespoon freshly squeezed lemon juice

SALAD

1 pound (500 g) lamb steak, cut from the fillet

2 tablespoons extra-virgin olive oil

1 pound (500 g) green beans

3 cups (150 g) baby spinach

½ cup (50 g) Kalamata olives, rinsed and drained

1 pound (500 g) cherry tomatoes, halved

ORANGE DRESSING

¼ cup (60 ml) sherry vinegar

¼ cup (60 ml) orange juice

2 tablespoons extra-virgin olive oil

1 small red onion, finely chopped

1 teaspoon brown sugar
  Salt and freshly ground black pepper

1. **To prepare the rosemary and lemon marinade,** pound the rosemary, oregano, peppercorns, and lemon zest and juice with a pestle and mortar to make a paste.

2. **Place** the lamb in a shallow glass or ceramic dish. Brush with the oil, then rub with the marinade. Cover the dish and marinate in the refrigerator for 12 hours or overnight.

3. **To prepare the orange dressing,** whisk the sherry vinegar, orange juice, oil, onion, brown sugar, salt, and pepper in small bowl.

4. **Cook** the green beans in lightly salted boiling water until crunchy-tender, 2–3 minutes. Drain and let cool.

5. **To prepare the salad,** preheat a grill pan or barbecue to high heat. Place the lamb in the pan or on the barbecue. Cook to taste: 3–5 minutes each side for medium-rare. Remove from the heat. Cover with aluminum foil and rest for 10 minutes.

6. **Slice** the lamb. Put in a bowl and drizzle with half the dressing. Toss to combine.

7. **Combine** the spinach, olives, tomatoes, and green beans in a bowl. Toss to combine. Arrange on six serving dishes and top with the lamb. Drizzle with the dressing and serve.

AMOUNT PER SERVING	257 CALORIES 12%	20g PROTEIN 43%	16g FAT 20%	4g FIBER 16%	9g CARBS 7%	0.6g SALT 9%
NUTRITION FACTS **PERCENT DAILY VALUES** (based on 2 000 calories)						

lamb salad with tzatziki

Tzatziki is a classic Greek yogurt dip. It can be served with pita bread as an appetizer or as an accompaniment to more substantial meat and fish dishes.

 Serves 4

 10 minutes

 6–10 minutes

 1

LAMB SALAD

3	tablespoons extra-virgin olive oil
1	pound (500 g) lamb steak, cut from the fillet
16	cherry tomatoes, halved
2	bunches arugula (rocket)
	Salt and freshly ground black pepper

TZATZIKI

1	cup (250 ml) plain Greek-style yogurt
2	cloves garlic, finely chopped
1	small cucumber, peeled and cut into small dice
1	tablespoon finely chopped fresh mint
1	tablespoon extra-virgin olive oil
1	tablespoon freshly squeezed lemon juice

1. **To prepare the lamb salad,** preheat a grill pan or barbecue to high heat. Place the lamb in the pan or on the barbecue. Cook to taste: 3–5 minutes each side for medium-rare.

2. **Put** the arugula and tomatoes on a large serving dish. Slice the lamb and place over the salad. Season with salt and pepper.

3. **To prepare the tzatziki,** combine the yogurt, garlic, cucumber, mint, oil, and lemon juice in a bowl and mix well.

4. **Serve** the lamb salad warm with tzatziki spooned over the top.

AMOUNT PER SERVING	376	30g	27g	1g	4g	0.1g
NUTRITION FACTS	**CALORIES**	**PROTEIN**	**FAT**	**FIBER**	**CARBS**	**SALT**
PERCENT DAILY VALUES (based on 2000 calories)	18%	65%	33%	4%	3%	2%

If you liked this recipe, you will love these as well.

lamb & orange **couscous salad**
274

barbecued lamb salad
276

lamb salad with herbs
278

Fruity Finishes

fruit salad with lemon syrup

This fresh fruit salad can be made the day before serving and kept in the refrigerator. If it has been in the refrigerator for several hours, take it out about 15 minutes before serving.

Serves 4

15 minutes

1–2 hours

2 minutes

1

$\frac{1}{3}$ cup (90 ml) freshly squeezed lemon juice

$\frac{1}{3}$ cup (90 ml) water

2 tablespoons sugar

2 bananas, sliced

$\frac{1}{2}$ small pineapple, peeled, cored, and cut into chunks

2 cups (300 g) strawberries, sliced

4 passion fruit

3 tablespoons shredded (desiccated) coconut

1. **Combine** the lemon juice, water, and sugar in a small saucepan. Bring to a boil, then simmer over low heat for 2 minutes. Let cool to room temperature.

2. **Combine** the bananas, pineapple, and strawberries in a large bowl. Cut the passion fruit in half and scoop the pulp into the bowl. Drizzle with the syrup and toss gently.

3. **Chill** in the refrigerator for 1–2 hours. Sprinkle with the coconut just before serving.

AMOUNT PER SERVING	157	2g	6g	4g	25g	0g
NUTRITION FACTS	**CALORIES**	**PROTEIN**	**FAT**	**FIBER**	**CARBS**	**SALT**
PERCENT DAILY VALUES (based on 2 000 calories)	8%	4%	7%	16%	19%	0%

If you liked this recipe, you will love these as well.

fruit salad with raspberry sauce

288

fresh fruit salad in pineapple shells

292

mango with berries

When buying mangoes, make sure they have a fragrant, fruity aroma and yield only slightly to pressure from your thumb. They will ripen sitting on a kitchen counter or tucked away in a paper bag.

 Serves 4

🕐 10 minutes

🌡 1–2 hours

🍸 1

2	mangoes, peeled and diced
2	cups (300 g) strawberries, sliced
2	cups (300 g) raspberries, blackberries, or blueberries, or any combination of berry fruits

1	tablespoon superfine (caster) sugar
2	tablespoons dry white wine Greek yogurt or crème fraîche, to serve

1. **Combine** the mangoes and all the berries in a medium bowl.

2. **Sprinkle** with the sugar and drizzle with the wine. Toss well.

3. **Chill** in the refrigerator for 1–2 hours.

4. **Serve cold,** with the Greek yogurt or crème fraîche passed separately.

AMOUNT PER SERVING	91	2g	0g	7g	20g	0g
NUTRITION FACTS	**CALORIES**	**PROTEIN**	**FAT**	**FIBER**	**CARBS**	**SALT**
PERCENT DAILY VALUES (based on 2000 calories)	4%	4%	0%	28%	15%	0%

If you liked this recipe, you will love these as well.

berry fruit salad

302

fruit salad in spicy lime syrup

308

fruit salad with raspberry sauce

Freeze raspberries when they are plentiful in the summer by spreading them out on a baking sheet and freezing individually. When frozen, transfer to small containers.

Serves 6

15 minutes

1–2 hours

1

RASPBERRY SAUCE

2 cups (300 g) fresh or frozen raspberries (thawed, if frozen)

2 tablespoons superfine (caster) sugar

1 tablespoon freshly squeezed lemon juice

FRUIT SALAD

1½ pounds (750 g) mixed seasonal fruit, such as apples, peaches, pears, grapes, melons, mandarins or tangerines, kiwi fruit, sliced or chopped

2 bananas, sliced

2 tablespoons freshly squeezed lemon juice

1. **To prepare the raspberry sauce,** combine the raspberries, sugar, and 1 tablespoon of lemon juice in a small bowl and mash with a fork until liquid and the sugar has dissolved.

2. **Chill** in the refrigerator for 1–2 hours.

3. **To prepare the fruit salad,** combine the mixed fruit and bananas in a fruit salad bowl and drizzle with the lemon juice. This will stop the fruit from darkening and also heighten its natural flavors.

4. **Chill** in the refrigerator until ready to serve with the raspberry sauce spooned over the top.

AMOUNT PER SERVING NUTRITION FACTS PERCENT DAILY VALUES (based on 2000 calories)	300 CALORIES 14%	2g PROTEIN 4%	13g FAT 16%	7g FIBER 28%	47g CARBS 36%	0g SALT 0%

If you liked this recipe, you will love these as well.

mango with berries

286

fruit salad cups

300

melon & lychee salad

If serving this dish to children, replace the sweet white wine with good-quality white grape juice.

 Serves 4

 10 minutes

 2–3 hours

 1

1	cantaloupe (rock) melon, peeled, seeded, and cubed
1	(20-ounce/600-g) can lychees, drained
2	tablespoons finely chopped fresh mint
¾	cup (180 ml) sweet white wine

1. **Combine** the melon, lychees, and mint in a large bowl. Drizzle with the wine and toss well.

2. **Chill** for 2–3 hours before serving.

AMOUNT PER SERVING	161	2g	0g	4g	31g	0g
NUTRITION FACTS	CALORIES	PROTEIN	FAT	FIBER	CARBS	SALT
PERCENT DAILY VALUES (based on 2000 calories)	8%	4%	0%	16%	24%	0%

If you liked this recipe, you will love these as well.

watermelon salad

74

summer fruit kebabs with chocolate

294

fresh fruit salad
in pineapple shells

Choose an attractive, evenly shaped large pineapple for this recipe.

 Serves 4

 20 minutes

 2 hours

 1

1	pineapple
2	mangoes, peeled and diced
4	kiwi fruit, peeled and diced
2	oranges, peeled and segmented
6	passion fruit, halved and pulp removed
1/3	cup (90 ml) Cointreau or other orange-flavored liqueur
4	tablespoons confectioners' (icing) sugar
1	cup (150 g) fresh raspberries
1	tablespoon fresh mint leaves, chopped
1 1/2	cups (375 ml) plain yogurt

1. **Cut** the pineapple in half lengthwise and, using a small sharp knife, make an incision around the perimeter 1 inch (2.5 cm) in from the skin on each half. Remove the flesh with a knife and spoon, leaving the shells intact. Slice the pineapple flesh into small pieces, discarding the tough core.

2. **Put** the pineapple flesh in a large bowl. Add the mangoes, kiwi fruit, oranges, and passion fruit, stirring to combine.

3. **Mix** the Cointreau and confectioners' sugar in a small bowl and pour over the fruit. Add the raspberries and mint and stir gently to combine.

4. **Spoon** the fruit salad into the pineapple shells and refrigerate for 2 hours to allow the flavors to infuse.

5. **Serve** with the yogurt passed separately.

AMOUNT PER SERVING	310	8g	2g	7g	56g	0.2g
NUTRITION FACTS	CALORIES	PROTEIN	FAT	FIBER	CARBS	SALT
PERCENT DAILY VALUES (based on 2000 calories)	15%	17%	2%	28%	43%	4%

If you liked this recipe, you will love these as well.

fruit salad in spicy lime syrup

308

exotic fruit salad with roquefort sauce

312

summer fruit kebabs
with chocolate sauce

Fresh fruit goes surprisingly well with chocolate. Vary the fruit according to the season.

 Serves 6

30 minutes

2 hours

3	firm ripe peaches, pitted and cut into chunks
3	firm ripe nectarines, pitted and cut into chunks
3	firm ripe apricots, pitted and cut into chunks

2	tablespoons superfine (caster) sugar
½	cup (125 ml) dry white wine
8	ounces (250 g) milk chocolate, coarsely chopped

1

1. **Combine** the peaches, nectarines, and apricots in a medium bowl. Sprinkle with the sugar and drizzle with the wine. Toss well to combine. Chill in the refrigerator for 2 hours.

2. **Drain** the fruit and thread onto metal skewers. Arrange on six individual serving plates.

3. **Melt** the chocolate in a double boiler over barely simmering water.

4. **Drizzle** the melted chocolate over the fruit and serve.

AMOUNT PER SERVING	267	4g	23g	2g	36g	0.1g
NUTRITION FACTS	CALORIES	PROTEIN	FAT	FIBER	CARBS	SALT
PERCENT DAILY VALUES (based on 2000 calories)	13%	9%	28%	8%	28%	2%

If you liked this recipe, you will love these as well.

melon, zucchini & pancetta **salad**

melon & lychee **salad**

28

290

oranges in red wine

Choose organic oranges that have not been waxed or treated in any way for this recipe.

 Serves 6

 10 minutes

 1 hour

 5 minutes

 1

1	cup (250 ml) dry red wine	2	whole cloves
1	cup (250 ml) water	2	slices lemon
½	cup (100 g) sugar	6	organic oranges
1	cinnamon stick		

1. **Combine** the wine, water, sugar, cinnamon, cloves, and lemon in a saucepan. Bring to a boil, stirring frequently, then lower the heat and simmer for 3 minutes.

2. **Use a lemon zester** to remove about 2 tablespoons of zest (orange part only) from the oranges. Peel the rest, removing all the white pith. Segment the fruit, removing the membranes.

3. **Place** the segments of orange and the zest in the hot syrup. Let cool to room temperature.

4. **Chill** in the refrigerator for 1 hour before serving.

AMOUNT PER SERVING	142 CALORIES	2g PROTEIN	0g FAT	2g FIBER	29g CARBS	0g SALT
NUTRITION FACTS PERCENT DAILY VALUES (based on 2 000 calories)	7%	4%	0%	8%	22%	0%

If you liked this recipe, you will love these as well.

champagne strawberries

298

fresh fruit piña colada

310

champagne strawberries

Serve these strawberries on a hot summer's day. For a change, replace the champagne with the same quantity of chilled sparkling Italian prosecco.

 Serves 4

 5 minutes

 2 hours

3 cups (500 g) strawberries, halved

¼ cup (60 ml) orange-flavored liqueur

2 cups (500 ml) chilled, very dry champagne

 1

1. **Put** the strawberries in a medium glass bowl and drizzle with the orange-flavored liqueur. Pour 1 cup (250 ml) of champagne into the bowl. Cover and chill in the refrigerator for 2 hours.

2. **Divide** the strawberries and their juices evenly among four serving glasses. Pour the remaining champagne over the top and serve.

AMOUNT PER SERVING	CALORIES	PROTEIN	FAT	FIBER	CARBS	SALT
NUTRITION FACTS	176	1g	0g	3g	13g	0g
PERCENT DAILY VALUES (based on 2 000 calories)	8%	2%	0%	12%	10%	0%

If you liked this recipe, you will love these as well.

fruit salad with lemon syrup

284

oranges in red wine

296

fruit salad cups

Serve these pretty fruit cups as a quick and healthy dessert during the summer.

 Serves 6

 15 minutes

 1–2 hours

 1

2 ripe peaches, pitted and sliced

8 ripe apricots, pitted and sliced

2 ripe nectarines, pitted and sliced

1 mango, peeled, pitted, and cut into small pieces

12 ounces (350 g) cherries, pitted and halved

1 tablespoon superfine (caster) sugar

¼ cup (60 ml) sweet dessert wine

1 tablespoon finely chopped fresh mint, to garnish

1. **Combine** the peaches, apricots, nectarines, mango, and cherries in a large bowl.

2. **Sprinkle** the sugar over the fruit and drizzle with the wine. Chill in the refrigerator for 1–2 hours.

3. **Spoon** the fruit and juices into six individual serving cups. Garnish with the mint and serve.

AMOUNT PER SERVING	131 CALORIES	3g PROTEIN	0g FAT	3g FIBER	29g CARBS	0g SALT
NUTRITION FACTS PERCENT DAILY VALUES (based on 2000 calories)	6%	7%	0%	12%	22%	0%

If you liked this recipe, you will love these as well.

shrimp & mango salad

206

mango with berries

286

berry fruit salad

Use any combination of fresh, in-season berry fruit for this salad.

 Serves 6

10 minutes

2–3 hours

5 minutes

1

1¼	cups (300 ml) dry white wine
¼	cup (50 g) superfine (caster) sugar
1	teaspoon finely grated lemon zest

1	clove
2	cups (300 g) strawberries, sliced
2	cups (300 g) raspberries
1	cup (150 g) blackberries
1	cup (120 g) blackcurrants

1. Combine the wine, sugar, lemon zest, and clove in a small saucepan. Bring to a boil, then simmer until the sugar is dissolved, 1–2 minutes. Remove from the heat and let cool a little.

2. Combine the strawberries, raspberries, blackberries, and blackcurrants in a serving bowl. Pour the warm syrup over the top. Let cool to room temperature, about 1 hour.

3. Chill in the refrigerator for 1–2 hours. Remove the clove before serving.

AMOUNT PER SERVING	103 CALORIES	2g PROTEIN	0g FAT	8g FIBER	17g CARBS	0g SALT
NUTRITION FACTS						
PERCENT DAILY VALUES (based on 2000 calories)	5%	4%	0%	32%	13%	0%

If you liked this recipe, you will love these as well.

mango with berries

286

champagne strawberries

298

three fruit & honey salad

Choose a fruit- or flower-flavored honey to add extra spice to this salad.

 Serves 4

10 minutes

1 hour

1

1	cantaloupe (rock) melon, peeled, seeded, and cut into small cubes
2	kiwi fruit, peeled and sliced
1	cup (150 g) small seedless black grapes

3	tablespoons freshly squeezed lime juice
1	tablespoon honey
½	teaspoon ground cinnamon
	Lime zest, to garnish

1. **Combine** the melon, kiwi fruit, and grapes in a serving bowl.

2. **Whisk** the lime juice, honey, and cinnamon in a small bowl. Drizzle over the fruit and chill in the refrigerator for 1 hour.

3. **Garnish** the fruit with the lime zest and serve.

AMOUNT PER SERVING	92	1g	0g	2g	22g	0.1g
NUTRITION FACTS	CALORIES	PROTEIN	FAT	FIBER	CARBS	SALT
PERCENT DAILY VALUES (based on 2000 calories)	4%	2%	0%	8%	17%	2%

If you liked this recipe, you will love these as well.

cheese, pear & kiwi fruit salad

26

kiwi fruit & mushroom salad

30

sweet chile & pineapple salad

When perfectly ripe and ready to eat, a pineapple smells sweet. If it has no scent, then it's not ripe. If it smells strongly and slightly musty, then it's overripe.

 Serves 6

5 minutes

3–4 minutes

¼ cup (60 g) butter

2 tablespoons light brown sugar

1 fresh red chile, seeded and finely chopped

1 ripe pineapple, peeled, cored, and sliced

½ cup (125 ml) heavy (double) cream, to serve

1

1. **Combine** the butter, brown sugar, and chile in a large frying pan over medium heat.

2. **Add** the pineapple and sauté until the fruit is coated in the butter mixture and heated through, 3–4 minutes.

3. **Whip** the cream until thick. Serve the fruit hot with the cream passed separately.

AMOUNT PER SERVING NUTRITION FACTS PERCENT DAILY VALUES (based on 2000 calories)	230 CALORIES 11%	1g PROTEIN 2%	20g FAT 25%	1g FIBER 4%	14g CARBS 11%	0.1g SALT 2%

If you liked this recipe, you will love these as well.

arugula & pineapple salad

58

fresh fruit salad in pineapple shells

292

fruit salad in spicy lime syrup

The tamarind concentrate used in the syrup has a tangy sweet-and-sour flavor. If you can't find tamarind, substitute with fresh lemon or lime juice mixed with a pinch of brown sugar.

Serves 4

15 minutes

10 minutes

5 minutes

1

SPICY LIME SYRUP
1	cup (150 g) grated palm sugar or light brown sugar
1/3	cup (90 ml) water
	Finely grated zest of 1 lime
2	tablespoons freshly squeezed lime juice
1	teaspoon tamarind concentrate
1	fresh red chile, seeded and finely chopped

FRUIT SALAD
1	small pineapple, peeled, cored, and cut into small pieces
1	mango, peeled, pitted, and cut into small pieces
1	banana, sliced
1	apple, cored and diced
1	cucumber, peeled and diced
12	fresh lychees, peeled, seeded, and chopped

1. To prepare the spicy lime syrup, combine the sugar, water, and lime zest and juice in a small saucepan. Bring to a boil, then simmer over low heat for 5 minutes. Let cool for 10 minutes.

2. Add the tamarind concentrate and chile and stir to combine.

3. Combine the pineapple, mango, banana, apple, cucumber, and lychees in a serving bowl. Pour the syrup over the top and toss gently before serving.

AMOUNT PER SERVING	248	1g	0g	3g	64g	0.1g
NUTRITION FACTS	CALORIES	PROTEIN	FAT	FIBER	CARBS	SALT
PERCENT DAILY VALUES (based on 2000 calories)	12%	2%	0%	12%	49%	2%

If you liked this recipe, you will love these as well.

fruit salad with lemon syrup

284

champagne strawberries

298

fresh fruit piña colada

For this salad—and all the other fresh fruit salads in this chapter—choose the best-quality, freshest, in-season fruit available. The outcome of the dish depends entirely on the quality of the fruit.

 Serves 4

10 minutes

1 hour

1

1	pineapple, peeled, cored, and cut into small pieces
1	mango, peeled, pitted, and cut into small cubes
½	papaya, peeled, seeded, and cut into small cubes

¼	cup (60 ml) coconut milk
¼	cup (60 ml) pineapple juice
2	tablespoons dark rum
	Toasted coconut, to garnish

1. **Combine** the pineapple, mango, and papaya in a serving bowl.

2. **Whisk** the coconut milk, pineapple juice, and rum in a small bowl. Pour over the fruit and mix gently. Chill in the refrigerator for at least 1 hour.

3. **Garnish** the salad with the toasted coconut just before serving.

AMOUNT PER SERVING	114	1g	3g	2g	19g	0.1g
NUTRITION FACTS	**CALORIES**	**PROTEIN**	**FAT**	**FIBER**	**CARBS**	**SALT**
PERCENT DAILY VALUES (based on 2 000 calories)	5%	2%	4%	8%	15%	2%

If you liked this recipe, you will love these as well.

oranges in red wine

296

champagne strawberries

298

sweet chile & pineapple salad

306

exotic fruit salad
with roquefort sauce

If desired, serve this fruit salad in the avocado skins. Choose avocados with unmarked skins and slice in half. Remove the pit and flesh, leaving a thick enough layer of flesh in the skin to create a natural serving bowl.

 Serves 4

 20 minutes

 2

FRUIT SALAD

2   avocados, peeled, pitted, and cut into small cubes

Freshly squeezed juice of 1 lemon

1   mango, peeled, pitted, and cut into small cubes

1   papaya, peeled, seeded, and cut into small cubes

2   kiwi fruit, peeled and cut into cubes

2   tablespoons dark rum

2   tablespoons pistachios

ROQUEFORT SAUCE

8   ounces (250 g) Roquefort cheese, crumbled

1/4   cup (60 ml) plain yogurt

1. **To prepare the fruit salad,** put the avocados in a large bowl. Drizzle with the lemon juice and mix gently.

2. **Add** the mango, papaya, and kiwi fruit. Stir in the rum.

3. **To prepare the Roquefort sauce,** combine the cheese and yogurt in a small bowl. Crush the cheese with a fork to make a smooth creamy sauce.

4. **Divide** the fruit salad among four serving dishes or place in the reserved avocado skins. Spoon the sauce over the top. Sprinkle with the pistachios and serve.

AMOUNT PER SERVING	443	16g	37g	4g	11g	2.6g
NUTRITION FACTS	CALORIES	PROTEIN	FAT	FIBER	CARBS	SALT
PERCENT DAILY VALUES (based on 2000 calories)	21%	35%	46%	16%	8%	44%

If you liked this recipe, you will love these as well.

blue cheese & pecan salad

22

pear, roquefort & radicchio salad

32

rice salad with apple & walnuts

164

dried fruit salad

Serve this hearty dried fruit salad during the cold winter months. It goes beautifully with a light vanilla custard, such as crème anglaise, or with whipped cream.

 Serves 6

10 minutes

12 hours

5 minutes

1

1	cup (180 g) dried apricots
1	cup (180 g) pitted prunes
½	cup (90 g) raisins
½	cup (90 g) dried peaches, cut in half
1	dried kiwi fruit, sliced

2	tablespoons freshly squeezed lemon juice
	Strip of lemon zest
½	cup (75 g) coarsely chopped almonds

1. Combine the dried apricots, prunes, raisins, peaches, kiwi fruit, and lemon juice and zest in a large glass or ceramic bowl. Pour in enough warm water to cover. Cover the bowl with plastic wrap (cling film) and let stand overnight. The dried fruit will plump and soften.

2. Strain the soaking liquid into a saucepan and return the fruit to the bowl. Add the lemon zest.

3. Prepare a syrup by bringing the soaking liquid to a boil and simmering over low heat for 5 minutes.

4. Pour the hot syrup over the fruit. Sprinkle with the almonds and serve.

AMOUNT PER SERVING	371	8g	11g	20g	63g	0.1g
NUTRITION FACTS	CALORIES	PROTEIN	FAT	FIBER	CARBS	SALT
PERCENT DAILY VALUES (based on 2 000 calories)	18%	17%	14%	80%	48%	2%

Index